1

SUPER-DOLLARS

by David Reinfurt

The British economist John Maynard Keynes knew that the value of money is based only in its circulation:

> The long age of Commodity Money has at last passed finally away before the age of Representative Money. Gold has ceased to be a coin, a hoard, a tangible claim to wealth, of which the value cannot slip away so long as the hand of the individual clutches the material stuff. It has become a much more abstract thing—just a standard of value; and it only keeps this nominal status by being handed round from time to time in quite small quantities amongst a group of Central Banks.
> (Keynes, *A Treatise on Money*, 1930)

While the Canadian Professor (and popular pundit) Marshall McLuhan properly identified money as a medium of exchange, translating one kind of work into another:

> Even today, money is a language for translating the work of the farmer into the work of the barber, doctor, engineer, or plumber. As a vast social metaphor, bridge, or translator, money—like writing—speeds up exchange and tightens the bonds of interdependence in any community. It gives great spatial extension and control to political organizations, just as writing does, or the calendar. It is action at a distance, both in space and in time. In a highly literate, frag-mented society, 'Time is money,' and money is the store of other people's time and effort.
> (McLuhan, *Understanding Media*, 1964)

But it took an ad-hoc movement of monetary hackers, with their Local Exchange Trading Systems, to identify another essential character-istic of money—we can make our own:

> Now here's the good news—all these problems can be fixed with money that's better designed. Money is just information, a way we measure what we trade, nothing of value in itself. And we can make it ourselves, to work as a complement to conventional money. Just a matter of design.
> (www.openmoney.org, *Open Money Manifesto*)

In a sublime synthesis of these three fundamental insights into the character of money, the government of The Democratic People's Republic of Korea has (allegedly) been manufacturing SuperDollars—impossibly accurate and indistinguishable counterfeit United States $100 bills. A BBC transcript from 2004 tells the story:

```
.........................................
THE SUPER DOLLAR
RECORDED FROM TRANSMISSION: BBC-1
DATE: 20:06:04
.........................................
```

VOICEOVER: For over a decade police forces across the world have been hunting a criminal cartel with a licence to print money. They've been distributing the highest quality counterfeit notes ever produced. The forgeries are so realistic that even the experts can't tell the difference.

DCI MARK SMITH: They would go through banks, they could be cashed at travel exchanges, bureau de change, they were that good, that well made, that sophisticated.

VOICEOVER: They're known as superdollars.

VOICE OF SILCOCK: This is made on the same paper, the same ink, the same little coloured flecks in the paper. There's that many of them in their economy, it's a joke.

VOICEOVER: For years superdollars have been passing unnoticed in banks throughout the world. Tonight, using exclusive surveillance footage, Panorama goes on the trail of the superdollar. We follow the tracks of a counterfeiting cartel around the world, from the rogue states of North Korea ...

KOREAN DEFECTOR: In North Korea this project is as important as the nuclear programme.

VOICEOVER: To the Russian capital, the hub of the operation where massive counterfeit deals take place on a regular basis.

VLADIMIR USKOV: Perhaps they didn't think they would be watched by the Special Services here.

VOICEOVER: And we confront one of the men who police believe to be involved in forcing the American Government to redesign its currency ...

DCI MARK SMITH: The quality of them was extraordinary. The first time that we actually recovered one of these new, big head style, $100 notes, a Secret Service agent spent a long time looking at it and couldn't determine that it actually was counterfeit.

VOICEOVER: But it isn't the first time the Secret Service has encountered a note of this type. In fact, they've been aware of them for a decade. Officially they're referred to as 'note family C 14342', privately agents call them superdollars. The first superdollars turned up in diplomatic bags of North Korean officials. Since then the North Korean regime have been implicated time after time in the distribution of the superdollar. It's one of the reasons the country has become a pariah state. The superdollar, according to some experts in North Korea, is a weapon against America.

BALBWA HWANG: North Korea has a state sponsored programme in which it is counterfeiting US dollars, and they do so with a dual purpose. The first is obviously the profits that that regime can earn immediately. But they also have a longer term strategy of attempting to destabilise the US economy ...

VOICEOVER: The whole operation depends on couriers. Those willing to carry the counterfeit around the world are paid thousands. In a Birmingham city centre hotel Silcock goes to meet an Irishman who's a veteran smuggler of counterfeit. But the hotel room is bugged. The police are about to hear from the inside just how the couriers operate.

[Police Sound Recording:]

VOICE OF HUGH TODD: But he wants to change the moody dollars into different currencies. Now I have to change those back into f----- dollars. So f--- this, so I sent him a big f----- bundle of f----- marks over to Dublin.

LAWN: The courier's name is Hugh Todd. He has a criminal record. He makes a fortune delivering currency all over the world.

VOICE OF TODD: I've got one hundred and eighty thousand f----- dollars, there's a big parcel like that, now I've go back out through those f----- customs and I'm watching, as you go, you know ... they're putting the bag through the scanner and there's a fella the far side and the odd one he stops and searches. I had the f----- things stuffed down here. Now I have 'em f----- stuffed down here, stuffed down everywhere. I have 'em in my f----- pants, I can feel one slipping down the f----- inside of my f----- pants, put my bag through, walked straight through, not searched, end of f----- story. I'm gone. I go into the f----- Irish bar, I go out, I go into the toilet, take my bag, like that, take all my dollars out, grand, put them all into the bag, sweet, I'm through.

That's it—the SuperDollars now circulate in the world economy. And although less than legal, the act of this counterfeiting reveals a few essential characteristics of money right now. Certainly, the SuperDollars' status as currency commands a closer look—like Keynes suggests, these notes circulate efficiently and gain value as a result; as McLuhan identifies, the SuperDollars become a medium of information and labor exchange; and as the Open Money Manifesto asserts, it is simply a matter of design (in this case, an indistinguishably precise copy.) In fact, according to *The Daily NK*, the SuperDollars are so meticulously produced and effective, that agents in Moscow sell them for $70 a piece!

As a result, the United States government must respond. So in a game of post-Cold War cat and mouse, the U.S. Bureau of Engraving and Printing will re-design, print and circulate a new $100 note every few years—each time more baroque in its design, precise in its manufacture and complex in its reproduction.

While at the same time, the overwhelming majority of financial transactions now involve electronic transfers where one account is credited and another debited, no cash required. This abstraction of money from any commodity basis or representative form together with its increasing transactional fluidity creates room for the circulation of private currencies. These are increasingly manifested as magnetic-swipe smart cards, radio-frequency ID chips, cellphone credits and encrypted electronic files. Hong Kong's Octopus, for example, may be used for transport and a variety of small purchases, and London's Oyster card recently replaced cash on the Underground system. Even the analogue New Hampshire State turnpike token issued for tolls may also be freely exchanged for a quarter within the state, though this hard currency's near-future fate seems to point the way for many others: the token features a depiction of the 'Old Man on the Mountain', which was also just recently minted to the back of the U.S. quarter, whose actual granite countenance has since fallen off.

UNWORKING BARTELBY THE SCRIVENER

by Dmitri Siegel

For Aristotle, all potential to be or do something is always potential not to be or not
to do, without which potentiality would
always have passed into actuality and would
be indistinguishable from it.
(Giorgio Agamben)

In *Bartelby the Scrivener: A Story of Wall Street*
Herman Melville recounts the tale of a humble
copyist Bartelby and his employer, a lawyer
whose name we never learn. Initially, Bartelby
performs remarkably, 'working day and night ...
as if long famished for something to copy.'
But his productivity stops suddenly. He does
not refuse to work; he does not leave; he simply
and without malice responds to every one of
the lawyer's requests, 'I prefer not to.' Bartelby
is a protagonist on strike. He embodies the
paradoxical power of strategies like passive
resistance, procrastination, refusal, and the
boycott. Although contemporary discourse
defines freedom as the ability to choose from
an array of circumscribed options, Bartelby
illustrates an altogether different kind of
freedom—the freedom to refrain.

Bartelby's inaction calls out to a common
humanity in the lawyer. He contemplates all
sorts of responses to Bartelby's intransigence:
compelling Bartelby to work, berating him,
forcing him to leave. But the scrivener's
language and his demeanor deter the lawyer.
He is captivated by Bartelby's, 'steadiness, his
freedom from all dissipation ... his great stillness,
his unalterableness of demeanor under all
circumstances.' Ultimately the lawyer moves his
entire office rather than contradict Bartelby's
preference not to.

In *American Fictions*, an examination of
the literary history of Manhattan, Elizabeth
Hardwick writes, 'Melville's structure is magical
because the lawyer creates Bartelby by allowing
him to be, a decision of nicely unprofessional
impracticality.' Hardwick's concept of
unprofessionality is critical: just as Bartelby
is defined by his un-work, the lawyer too must
compromise his work to engage with Bartelby.
He walks home 'suffering much from perplexity
and distress of mind.' He tolerates, he mulls,
but he does nothing. In fact, he says that each
refused request, 'only tended to lessen the
probability of my repeating the inadvertence.'
At one point Bartelby responds to a request
from the lawyer by suggesting that he walk
around the block two or three times; and the
lawyer does so, despite 'sundry twinges of
impotent rebellion against the mild effrontery
of this unaccountable scrivener.' Through his
own unworking, Bartelby manages to unwork
the lawyer as well.

It is no coincidence that Melville finds his
enthusiastically reluctant hero on Wall Street
—the capital of capital. Bartelby's contingency
emerges in direct opposition to work and as
Hardwick notes Wall Street in the 19th Century
was metonymic for the rising power of industry.
His job as a copyist reflects the abstraction of
productivity—money making money—that Wall
Street still embodies. Since then the locus of
work has been exploded into an ever-expanding,
diffuse cloud of productivity.

In his essay 'Free Time', philosopher Theodor
Adorno explains how our time away from work
has gradually been filled with economically
productive activities masquerading as leisure.
He explains how we become habituated to this
functionalization, so that when we have free
time we don't feel relaxed, but instead feel an
anxiety to function, that has become commonly
known as boredom. The limitless possibilities
have made us uncomfortable with doing nothing,
and at every turn there is a bit of work to ease
the discomfort.

Would Bartelby's steadfast evasion of work
even be possible today, when leisure activities
have been replaced by functional equivalents,
from home improvement to working-out?
Consider the popularity of the commercial grade
oven, the home office and the restaurant-style
kitchen. People come home after working an
eight-hour day and work on their website or
learn to apply an aged finish to their bathroom
walls. These used to be jobs but they have been
repackaged and redesigned as hobbies. In this

4

seamless flow of functionality even not working has become work.

Essential to this mechanization of leisure is a transformation of the idea of freedom. In 'Bartelby, or on Contingency' the philosopher Giorgio Agamben writes, 'As a scribe who has stopped writing, Bartelby is the extreme figure of the Nothing from which all creation derives; and at the same time, he constitutes the most implacable vindication of this Nothing as pure, absolute potentiality.' Agamben invokes Liebniz's idea of contingency, saying that Bartelby embodies, 'the contingent, which can be or not be and which coincides with the domain of human freedom in its opposition to necessity.'

Freedom is commonly understood as limitless potential—being able to do anything, but there is a fundamental ambiguity in the word 'anything'. It can mean 'any of the infinite possibilities' or 'any single one of the infinite possibilities.' In our culture of mass-customisation, social mobility, and democratization of luxury the latter interpretation has been successfully buried by the former. Choice and freedom are now understood as a network of sub-menus, a delirium of options for everything from toothpaste to living arrangements. T-shirts are made in every shade of irony. Jeans come in every bouquet of distress. The more we define ourselves by the things we choose the more potentiality is replaced by finite potential, contingency is replaced by customization, leisure is replaced by work, and rest is replaced by boredom.

The simple dichotomy of doing or not doing has been painted over with a phantasmagorical dancing image of the infinite. This is the 'freedom' that is celebrated in the rhetoric of politics, self-help, and art, but it glosses over the truth that is at the core of Melville's story: freedom disappears the moment that anything is transformed into something.

REFERENCES
—Adorno, Theodor. 'Free Time' (1977), in *The Culture Industry: Selected essays on mass culture*, (London: Routledge, 1991)
—Agamben, Giorgio. 'Bartelby, or On Contingency' from *Potentialities: Collected Essays in Philosophy* (Palo Alto: Stanford University Press, 1999)
—Hardwick, Elizabeth, 'Bartelby in Manhattan', in *American Fictions* (New York: Modern Library, 1999)
—Melville, Herman, *Bartelby, the Scrivener: A Story of Wall Street* (New York: Putnam's, 1853)

as in ANIMAL: Deleuze describes living an existence 'aux aguets', 'être aux aguets,' always being on the lookout, like an animal, like a writer, always looking back over one's shoulder. One writes for readers, 'for' meaning 'à l'attention de,' toward them, to their attention. But also, one writes for non-readers, that is, 'for' meaning 'in the place of.' Deleuze argues that thinking that writing is some tiny little private affair is shameful; writing means throwing oneself into a universal affair, be it a novel or philosophy.

as in BOIRE/BOISSON (DRINK): Drinking, he says, is a question of quantity. People make fun of addicts and alcoholics who pretend to be able to stop. What they want, is to reach the last drink/glass. An alcoholic never ceases to stop drinking, never ceases reaching the last drink. The last here means that he cannot stand to drink one more glass that particular day. It's the last in his power, versus the last beyond his power which would cause him to collapse. So the search is for the penultimate drink, the final drink … before starting the next day.

as in CULTURE: Deleuze attributes the crisis to three things: 1) Journalists have conquered the book form; 2) Writing has become the tiny affair of the individual; 3) The customers have changed: television's aren't viewers, but advertisers; publishing's not potential readers, but distributors. The result is rapid turnover, the regime of the best seller. But it's not all that serious, since there will always be either a parallel circuit for expression, or a black market.

What is a designer:
education and practice

by Norman Potter

a guide for students and teachers

1969

QUESTIONS WITHOUT QUESTION MARKS

A(nother) conversation with
Robin Kinross of Hyphen Press
by Stuart Bailey

I used to say 'typographer', in the days
when you had to say what you were in your
passport. It was a matter of slightly romantic
allegiance, because I never practised it in
the way that most people do. I also did a lot
of writing, and now I do a lot of editing—
which means, reading other people's writing,
and working with texts and working with
another designer. So I think now I'm an editor,
and in the Continental sense, or the French
sense of 'editeur'. That also means 'publisher'.
I'm pleased with that idea; it has some of
the same good qualities as 'typographer'.
It's not so much visual production as word
production. That's what I do.

*This is Robin's answer to a question from an
earlier interview with Petra Cerne Oven, originally
published in 1999 and currently available on the
Hyphen Press website [www.hyphenpress.co.uk].
Petra framed that piece by pointing out how
perfectly the hyphen represents Robin's practice,
both in the senses of carrying-on (the project
of modernist enlightenment) and break-ing
(from existing models of writing and publishing).
This new conversation attempts to act in the same
spirit, both continuing and diverging from the
previous discussion.*

*I first met Robin in 1993, somewhere around
the middle of my final year at the Department
of Typography & Graphic Communication
at The University of Reading, on the same course
Robin had completed himself some 20 years
earlier. A few interested students had invited
Robin to come and give an informal afternoon
talk, of which my time-bleached memory recalls
three things. The first was an introductory talk
loosely concerned with 'Locality', beginning*

*with some photographs of a small rural building
somewhere in what we then still thought of as
Continental Europe, a description of how its form
and materials were drawn from the area's history
and geography, and ending with a protracted
discussion about the precise typographic alignment
of three occurrences of the word 'Architecture'
on a Max Bill-designed book cover. This talk was
also memorable for the fact that, against Reading
protocol, Robin was both sat down and, apparently,
improvising. The second was a personal mini-
epiphany induced by the contents of a box Robin
had brought along: various publications and
ephemera as examples of local principles in
contemporary printed matter, mostly Dutch, and
approximately half of which were back issues of
the maverick architectural journal* Oase—Oasis!—
*designed by the then relatively uncelebrated
Karel Martens. The third was an absurdly
overheated discussion about the design of two wine
glasses placed in proximity to Robin towards the
end of the proceedings. In the closing sequence
a forgotten member of the audience is demanding
—with more irritation than seemed strictly
necessary—'What do you MEAN one is obviously
better than the other!? Which one!?', to which Robin
duly held up the one that was obviously better
than the other. At this point things started to make
a certain sense to me. In retrospect this was my
unofficial personal prologue to Robin's first major
work* Modern Typography, *which he had self-
published a couple of years beforehand.*

It's quite a strange book. It was the ideal
book for me, at that time. It had flaps
on the cover, and it was printed letterpress.
I think of it as 'the last letterpress book'.
The printer went out of business soon after
it was done. It was like leaving the sinking
ship of that technics: everything was going
down, but, well, we produced this book.

Stuart Bailey: In *Modern Typography* you describe
a social watershed around 1973 related to the
global oil crisis, and in your interview with Petra,
another in 1989 related to the dismantling of the
Berlin wall. In the seven years since that interview
I guess it's hard to deny another watershed in
2001 related to terrorism. Can you say something
about how you perceive the changes during each
of these periods has affected your publishing or
other activities?

Robin Kinross: My idea about the Zeitgeist,
and the way in which we see 'periods' as starting

and finishing, is that it is something that you tend to construct after the event. Yet, events like the oil-price crisis of 1973, or the fall of Communism in the autumn of 1989 and in the months following, and now 9/11, did all come with the sense of a powerful shock. You feel that you are living in history, whereas for the rest of your life, it's just days going by and getting on with your own immediate, personal concerns. But in those days of historical crisis, life thickens—the plot thickens. In 1973, quite a few of us in Britain felt that the world was going to end, or that we would be living in a different society, of scarcity and necessity. I found a confirmation of this in a book by Gilbert Adair—*Myths and Memories*, published in 1986—in which he says exactly that people thought the world was going to end then.

1980 and the time around then: I remember it as the coming of a new, radical conservatism, with Margaret Thatcher in Britain, and Ronald Reagan in the USA, and Helmut Kohl in what was still West Germany. It was also the coming of Postmodernism. I had started working with Norman Potter, an 'out and out Modernist', as I think he once put it. We went through this exercise of getting in touch with people that he had known or worked with in the 1950s and 1960s—people who might help with the new version of his book. Were they still modernists? Some of them had changed. Some of them were even becoming Postmodernists. (An architect like Terry Farrell in Britain, author of many grim Postmodern edifices, would be a good example of this.) It reminded me of a film of the 1950s, *The Invasion of the Bodysnatchers*. You look into the eyes of your girlfriend and see that she is different, has a blank look, has been taken over by some alien force.

With 9/11 and 2001, I don't feel the same sense of life thickening. Perhaps it's just that I want to refuse this as a reason for a change of practice. It's become a joke, almost. 'Why does this item cost more now?—'Because of 9/11.' The price of shipping books from Europe to the USA has gone up significantly in the last few years. I've been told that where previously a shipment was examined superficially—maybe just one crate was opened out of many—now every crate is opened and inspected. That takes time and costs money. I suppose I feel that the events of 9/11 and subsequently would never have happened if the USA had been following a more forthright, open, even-handed foreign policy, in Israel-Palestine, especially. So we are paying for this. I feel we

need to go on despite being told that everything is different now—as if these events hadn't happened. We need to assert some normality and continuity.

> There was something Anthony Froshaug once said to me: 'you've got the publishing bug as well.' He'd had it too. A lot of people have it. It's some wish to disseminate: to produce books or texts or information, and spread it around. Maybe it is a bug or a disease. There's something I do continually: if I see a newspaper article that I think will interest someone else, I cut it out and give it to them. Or I make two photocopies, and give one to that friend and the other to someone else. Maybe that's the publishing activity at its most basic: perhaps it's an instinct rather than a disease.

SB: Hyphen appears to be not only still afloat, but pretty stable, even introducing new series and so on. While arts publishing generally seems to be in some sort of crisis, driven to overproduction, blandness, and the steady erosion of standards by the nature of both print economies and middle management, how do you maintain this alternative?

RK: As far as my own publishing effort is concerned, the longer you go on, the more you can build on what you've done. So, in the last five or six years, books have begun to go out of print, and I've begun to make reprints or new editions. *What is a designer* is a case of this. In 2002 we made a fourth edition in a smaller format. It's now a true pocket book. Perhaps this is its final destination. (Norman Potter had died in 1995, so now there was no awkward author to dispute the new format.) Another way of consolidating is selling rights to translated editions, and this has begun to happen now. It's very gratifying, and it helps the economy of the effort, with royalties beginning to come in with no further expenses or effort. Norman used to say, half seriously, 'what about the Chinese market?' Last week I got an offer for a Chinese translation of one of the books—unfortunately not *What is a designer*.

This leads on to a theme that I'd like to expand on, both in the publishing, and perhaps in this interview. This is the reprinting of existing work, and the rediscovery of old texts. It was how I started, by bringing Potter's book back into existence. We did it again with Harry Carter's book *A View of Early Typography*, which appeared in a Hyphen edition in 2002, having been published by Oxford University Press in 1969, and then lying out of print for many years. This act of re-publication goes against the grain of publishing as it now exists in the bland corporate sphere. The tendency of large-scale publishing is to forget the old ones and to reinvent them. To some extent, this is understandable. The subject matter, the methods, the technologies, may all have changed. A book will begin to look dated in its design, and the firm that holds rights in it may not want to resuscitate it as it stands. It seems to me a noble and useful project to bring books back to life: at least, those books that still have life in them. Small, marginal publishers are well placed to do that.

> I suffer from a certain moralism. I've tended to make moral arguments, such as: 'this person has been neglected and should be better known', or 'this is an honest man; the world is full of dishonest people who are always in the headlines, why don't we pay attention to the ones who aren't in the headlines.

SB: These notions of reference and renewal seem particularly timely. A few years ago Will Holder and I produced a small-run publication called *Tourette's* in which a tiny editorial note proposed: 'A lot has been said already, and if we all keep trying to repeat and improve ourselves in new ways, some of the nicest things might get lost in the resulting pile'; and in DDD12, Ben Watson and Esther Leslie wrote 'that which burns brightest burns most briefly, and in true modernist fashion brilliance must be but fleeting, timely, not eternal, a coincidence of moment, viewer and object.' There's something about both these quotes which affirms for me the idea of design as verb rather than noun—as a way of thinking rather than a material end product. When teaching I always find myself talking about the importance of realising the thing you end up with at the close of a project is merely one possible cut-off point of the design, and that there still remain any number of potential directions or possibilities for revision. This attitude of continuation was always embodied for me by the fact that Potter's *What is a designer* has no question mark. Perhaps you could unpack that title—and that thought!—for me.

RK: The title of Norman's book is poetic, suggestive, like everything he wrote. In my mind, it means 'this is what I think design is; well, let's try it this way and see where we get to.' Often bookshops or people who ask about the book refer to it as 'What is a designer?' with a question mark.

One colleague said it sounded like a careers advice text ('What is Psychiatric Nursing?'). But the lack of a question mark in the title makes all the difference. There is also the disjunction between 'what' and 'designer'. 'Who is a designer' or 'what is design'—either of those would be expected, but not this mixture of the impersonal and the personal. Then he plays a nice trick by calling the first chapter 'What is a designer?', with the emphasis on 'is'. We might have rammed this home by calling that chapter 'So, what is a designer, anyway?'

> I remember a long conversation with Norman Potter and a common friend, in her garden, one summer evening. Norman persuaded me. He was a brilliant arguer: fantastically strong in reasoning. He said something like: 'You have to publish it yourself. That's part of the content.' He thought that the book itself should be a kind of demonstration: an existential acting-out. Perhaps it's like asking a composer if they can play the piece that they have composed. It's an exaggeration, but publishing the book myself was a kind of validation of what I was arguing. Certainly the form of the book, the design of it—although now I'm not happy with that—I felt this had to confirm or support the arguments of the book.

SB: Could you relate some of the particular lessons learned through publishing, editing or designing of your own books? Have you refined your approach? For example, was the recent introduction of Hyphen books in standardised formats a reaction to your experience publishing the earlier autonomous books?

RK: The trouble with my book *Modern Typography*, in its first edition, was, I came to think, in its own design. The design suffered from being too pondered: the process went on too long, without anyone pressing me to finish it. And also the whole process of making it was quite introverted. The wide left margin was meant to have pictures in it, to begin with. Then I decided not to use marginal pictures, but somehow forgot that this could mean that the left margin could be reduced, or that the page size could become smaller. And so on. Looking back at it now, I think the design of the book has a certain visible intention and a naivety or innocence. It's an attempt to make books in a certain way. That feels good, even if the details seem mostly wrong. In the second edition, we used a more modest format, and it's more standardised in its design. It's less about the design and more about the content.

9

The surprising thing to me is that the Hyphen books are, I think, rather various in appearance and style. So far it has been like a journey, meeting people along the way, walking with them a bit, and taking paths that they suggest—which wouldn't have happened if I'd been walking alone, or according to a foreseen plan. It's like the essay form, which is the way of writing that I feel most comfortable with: you start out not knowing where you will go, and the form of the piece tends to be made up as you go. T.W. Adorno expounds all this in his wonderful piece 'The essay as form', which I read a few years ago with a great sense of confirmation.

> I'm very suspicious of separated history [...] What I want more is 'this poster from 1817 was made because of the great interest in—whatever the topic is, and there was a development in printing technique which made it possible to make it so big, and there was an enlightened customer who had this much money to spend, but he ran out of money and this is why there were only ...' In other words, a more realistic level of discussion. I've seen that students who don't think they are interested in history are actually interested in this kind of discussion: they are drawn into it; it connects to their own experience.

SB: The retrospective rationalising and organising of history we mentioned earlier must apply at a smaller scale to Hyphen Press too, in the sense you describe of there having never been any masterplan, that you just 'fell into' publishing through certain friendships or the love of particular works. I might argue that an aspect of the modernism your publishing circumscribes is the very lack of any agenda or expectations, only a set of moral working principles, and that it's precisely this lack of presumption that breathes life into the work. Is it important to maintain a sense of unknowing, of making it up as you go along? Have you ever felt your work was becoming too predictable or out of breath?

RK: Yes, and more often recently. To do fresh work, as we're saying, you do need to take a step back and pause. Then something different can happen. It's perhaps what distinguishes mere journalism or 'journeyman work' from more substantial writing or production. As a writer, eventually you reach some point where the words just pour out without difficulty, as fast as you can type them. To write for a living, which usually means writing journalism, you do need to reach this state.

But this is dangerous, because of the risk that you start to 'run on empty'—repeat ideas, phrases, formulations. Or you just become a machine for rehashing given material: putting pieces together out of quotes from people that you phone or meet. This was one reason why I decided to stop a rather intensive phase of journalism at the end of the 1980s, and put most of my effort into something more long-lasting: making books. I felt I had begun to repeat myself.

Norman Potter's work, and the experience of working with him, was and still is formative for me. I remember he once told me he never gave the same lecture twice. Of course this is disastrous for an easy, lucrative career as a speaker on the conference circuit. But he felt that to keep it lively you had to do it differently every time, according to the circumstances of the audience, the venue, the occasion. I don't give many talks anyway, but on the one or two occasions where I've repeated a lecture, it's always gone wrong. Much better to do each one fresh. There is more work of preparation, but on the day you have a charge of fresh energy that isn't there with repetition.

> There were people making these manifestos, even, about what graphic design could or should be. My attempt was to discuss the arguments, and not the design that followed, or was said to follow, from the arguments. I thought the arguments were bad ones, and false. If you see what you think is confusion, and you think you know what the muddle is, then you go and say to the people saying these things 'look, you're confused'. [laughs] I begin to think that people found that quite strange. In graphic design, that is not so expected. Of course in philosophy or in history or other such areas, it happens all the time. That's partly what philosophy is: people saying 'look, this is what's going on here'.

SB: In his book *A Year (With Swollen Appendices)* Brian Eno writes the following in relation to the notion of abandoning what he calls 'axis thinking': 'It's extraordinary that when the Berlin Wall came down everyone assumed that the whole world was about to become one big market economy running on the same set of rules. What happened instead was that the old dualism Communism/Capitalism was revealed to conceal a host of possible hybrids. Now only the most ideological governments (England, Cuba) still retain their fundamentalist commitment to one end of the continuum: most governments are experimenting vigorously with

Norman Potter

What is a designer
: things . places . messages

A new, revised, and much extended edition
of this standard work for those who study &
practise architecture and design

" All students and teachers should read it " - Design

1980

Norman Potter

What is a designer
: things . places . messages

3 third edition of 'a classic'
'a text that will be returned to
by generation after generation'

1989

Norman Potter
What is a designer
: things . places . messages

fourth edition

2002

Robin Kinross **Modern typography**
an essay in critical history

1992

Robin Kinross
Modern typography
an essay in critical history

2004

Robin Kinross Fellow readers
notes on multiplied language

bubble of meaning. Something
could mean anything, and so
quickly it could only mean
nothing. And all of this echoed
the politics of the time: when a
sense of things in common was
displaced by free-for-all indi-
vidualism; and when individual liberty became reduced to
freedom to consume – if you
had the cash – watched over by
forces of the state.

1994

11

complicated customised blendings of market forces and state intervention.'

I'd argue that you can effectively apply this view to the prevailing condition of graphic design and typography (if not publishing), in the sense that there are no longer any general concerns about affiliation with some larger principle—the most recent obvious dualism being, of course, Modernism/Postmodernism. But I have to admit that feel a bit dualistic about it myself.

On one hand I think this is a good thing. One point I forgot to mention in my introduction about your Reading visit is that you also left behind your polemical 'More Light' article, originally published in 1993, which I'm guessing was some sort of precursor (maybe an angry younger brother) to your *Fellow Readers* pamphlet. There you write: 'An approach: Traditional? Modern? Postmodern? Forget those worries, and go back a step. Think what it is that you want to do. Think for yourself! Disregard preconceptions, models, influences.' In this sense, I think the current condition is halfway there —recent generations have forgotten those worries; the struggle now is towards the independent thinking part. This is also summed up nicely in a throwaway comment you make in answer to Petra's question about why graphic design stars (and by implication any kind of celebrity) are such a bad thing: because 'it stops people thinking for themselves'.

On the other hand I think it's a bad thing. The difficulty of writing about the breed of modernism you practise and, in doing so, promote, is that it's attitude rather than form, fluid rather than concrete, and therefore difficult for people to get a handle on, because 'readers' are used to having visual examples, when the form is typically 'read' as shorthand for the ideas. The problem isn't really a fundamental set of working principles itself, only when they become fundamentalist. I think it's desirable to work with an explicit set of beliefs—with preconceptions, models and influences—but I think the important thing is that they're worked through and out individually, over time and practice, not force-fed and swallowed. Without any principles at all you end up with some kind of vaguely existential tribal drift that Roger Bridgman lamented in his significantly-titled 'I'm Scared' (1962) and 'Who Cares?' (2002) pieces in the early issues of DDD.

All this is leading up to saying there's a quiet, modest radicality to Hyphen Press that I want to stick a flag in here, simply because

it's easy to miss. Radical has three basic meanings: 1. Arising from or going to a root or source; 2. Departing markedly from the usual or customary; and 3. Favouring or effecting fundamental or revolutionary changes in current practices, conditions, or institutions. Both the uncommon historical span in *Modern Typography* and its appendixed 'butterfly collection' of loaded images demonstrate all three: arising from the root of the subject, departing from the ways in which the subject is usually handled, and in doing so acting as a model towards changing current practice. *Fellow Readers* is another clear example: the immediacy of the text and brevity of its argument required a relatively speedy dissemination in order to participate in a contemporary argument, which informed the resurrection of the pamphlet format.

RK: There's a story I want to tell that perhaps qualifies some of the nice things you're suggesting about my lack of dogmatism and the suggestion that we've moved on beyond the polarities. I mention it in the spirit of self-criticism and self-questioning. And I have to mention Norman Potter again, though the attitude that he expressed is one that I share. A large part of the point of not having pictures in *What is a designer* is not to prejudice readers, to allow them to think for themselves. Occasionally Norman or I would encounter people who had read the book and thought it was wonderful, inspiring. They would show us their work, and it seemed really disappointing, just on the immediate level of appearance. We would think silently 'oh dear, they just don't get it'. So there can be a disjunction between ideas and products. You can have very good, noble intentions and still make uninteresting work. In the end, what you want is the thing itself, not the idea itself. What is an idea? An idea isn't really something to keep you alive and healthy. But then again, maybe this is to fall into polarisation. What is most desirable is when these poles disappear. What is produced is some fusion or embodiment. It has a richness.

> It's a familiar paradox. You develop a system. In principle you can tell other people how to do the work. But when it comes to it, you realise that it's actually a little bit more complicated. You begin to think that it needs the original people to do it right. In other words, it's more like art than it is like science or method. What that art is is not exactly mysterious, but it's a subtle matter.

SB: This brings me back to the standardisation question again. In Petra's interview you recalled Norman Potter urging you to self-publish *Modern Typography* because the self-publishing—the DIY—was 'part of the argument'. Are the recently-standardised Hyphen formats and typeface (Fred Smeijers' Arnhem) be considered a model in the same way? Why arrive at this point now, after a couple of decades of every book assuming a different form? I was thinking recently about how the majority of graphic design and typography I appreciate are those which feel 'standardised' because they seem to have been designed by time rather than people. I'm thinking of *The Guardian*, *The New York Times*, *The New Yorker*, *Time Out*, even: all the result of a collective effort, spanning generations and technics, rather than springing from some single genius moment. This might be considered, like the revisiting and refining existing books that we discussed earlier, in terms of publishing—and designing—as palimpsest.

RK: Perhaps it's part of this feeling of doing it for the long term. But certainly to fix the materials and the formats gives a freedom that I enjoy. If the format, the paper, the binding method, the typeface, and so on, are already given—then you are free to get on with making the book. You can play variations on the given materials. Maybe a certain title will demand a different kind of paper. But then you have a starting point from which to depart, and you are no longer facing the infinite—which of these five hundred possibilities shall I choose?

When I saw the typeface Arnhem, I thought, 'that's it'. At last there was a good, strong typeface that had been designed to be a digital thing from the start. So it could be superior to all the digitised versions of the hot-metal classics, which always feel like not very good translations that have lost something in the process. But Arnhem has the right balance of character and anonymity. Plus, of course, it had been made by a close colleague and friend, Fred Smeijers. So that felt good—to be joining hands with someone I knew well. Other contenders, such as Scala, designed by another good friend, Martin Majoor, had always seemed a bit too definite or stylish in their character. The typefaces I like most of all are the ones that just seem to be there without calling attention to themselves: newspaper typefaces, especially. I would have used Times and Plantin all the time if we were still doing metal typography.

Well, I come from an earlier culture, and an earlier generation. We were against heroes. As Brecht said, we wanted 'a land without heroes'. We thought that heroes only brought disasters. We were in favour of equality and collaboration, working without hierarchy. All those ideas.

SB: In slight relation to this, yet another quote, this time from John Berger's latest novel, *Here Is Where We Meet*, in which he describes the present condition as capitalist 'digital time' which continues forever uninterrupted through day and night, the seasons, birth and death: 'It's as indifferent to specificity and quality as money, and contrasts to the cyclical time of nature, of cold and warmth, of presence and feeling [...] digital time knows only vertical columns of ones and zeros, of cash flows and Dow indices. Within digital time, no whereabouts can be found or established; journeys no longer have a specific gravity of a destination. Destination has lost "its territory of experience".' It seems to me that the production of books works towards the maintenance of such a territory.

RK: Yes, that's one of the qualities that draws me to books. (Though, unfortunately, the more books you make, the less books you have time to read, or seem to be able to read.) But I cling to the idea that a book is for the long term. It will be there for as long as we're still above water. There's one part of the process of publishing that I enjoy especially. In the UK, one is asked to send one copy of any new book to the British Library, and copies also to the five 'legal deposit' libraries in Oxford, Cambridge, Edinburgh, Dublin, and Aberystwyth in Wales. When that's done, I always have the feeling that the book is there for ever. Even if every other copy is dispersed, or lost, or vandalised at Liverpool docks (as happened with one of our shipments to the USA), there will still be these six copies for the future.

I confess this is some sort of left-over religious attitude towards the holy book. It's also why I will never be able to throw any book into the rubbish bin, though some people I know can, or could, before the days of recycling of paper. That kind of reverence also means that you have to do everything to get the material of the book right, and free of error. (Though, unfortunately, the books I've made have often been quite full of mistakes—usually the result of giving ourselves unwise deadlines, to meet an exhibition opening or some such event.) Mistakes are the worst things in a book. Well, the books I want to make are the long-lasting ones. This becomes hard work in a culture in which books are being poured out every week, many of them put together very rapidly by people who want to 'do a book' as part of career advancement, whether as an academic or as a chat-show host.

> If you throw everything away, then you end up with nothing—or with complete freedom, with individuals saying 'I have a right to do this; don't say anything about me, because you're interfering with my personal rights'. I'm not sure how this really connects with the deconstruction arguments. But I think it does, because part of that argument is to say that each reader makes his or her own reading: 'don't interfere with the reading that I am making; it's mine.' So yes, to boil it down, that was what that was all about. And now I think it has passed on. What is fashionable now, in purely visual terms, is not that wild deconstruction. Things have changed.

SB: Finally, a question I've wanted to ask you for a while now. A few years ago, at the close of a piece I wrote about Maureen Mooren & Daniël van der Velden's redesign of *Archis* magazine, I quoted a section in *Modern Typography* where you suggest the prospect of 'an endless series of "modernisms", of multiple pastiche, and a sad, restless search for whatever might look new.' My conclusion was that this exactly described the form and attitude of *Archis* (though not in a necessarily negative way). At the time you hinted that I'd misunderstood your text. Could you say why, and whether you feel since then we've descended to the situation you anticipated there? Incidentally, I noticed you withdrew that entire 'Permanent restlessness' block of text that this came from in the second edition …

RK: *Archis* was extreme. I was amazed when I saw it, and could hardly believe what I was seeing. It looked rather Japanese, in that it was so largely based on imitation of existing forms (the design-styles of other magazines), with huge self-awareness, and fanatically precise details. But, yes, I did think it was awful. My blunt criticism of it would be that it was not just over-designed, but that the content was not well served. It was hard to know what the articles were about. Maybe this all mirrored the complexity of a world now saturated with media and representation. But in these circumstances, what is good to have is not a mirror, but the sharp knife of a clear

analysis. I remember that in the copies I borrowed from you, after you had written your article in *Eye* (no. 45, 2002), the one article I really wanted to read had been torn out—along the neatly serrated margin that all the pages had! Tear-out pages are, I feel, truly something that you might see in a nightmare.

When I wrote that passage in the first edition of *Modern Typography*, I was making a criticism, against the prospect of new modernisms that are just pastiches (the word was definitely meant as a put-down). It's perhaps interesting to try to make distinctions between things made now that go under the name of 'modernism'. For example, the architecture of Richard Meier is modernist, but I've always felt there was an element of pastiche in it, as if he knows too much about the history of modern architecture. His 'white architecture' has too many memories of the white buildings of heroic modernism, and it doesn't feel so appropriate in dull northern climates, such as you get in The Hague (the town hall there, designed by Meier's office). Perhaps this works better in the buildings for the Getty Center in Los Angeles. Also the kinds of buildings he has done—often large buildings, for rich clients —don't have the spare quality that animates the modern work that we tend to like best. The early work of Norman Foster had a fresh, spare modernist spirit, but now most of what the Foster office does feels rather dead, because of the size of it, the materials.

When I wrote the first edition of that book I did feel more embattled than I do now. It was the mid-1980s, and the time of ascendant post-modernism in all parts of life. It was a more polemical moment. Now a lot of that has passed, and the worst of post-modernism —the very superficial, badly made things, such as the Memphis furniture from Milan—now look laughable (if they ever didn't). I don't think I can explain why, but the situation feels better now. Objectively seen, it isn't. The galloping changes to the way our climate works, the degradation of the environment, the political crises all over the world—one could go on and on. But twentieth-century modernism, at its brightest and most hopeful, lived in the shadow of catastrophe—two huge wars. Rather than the 'sad and restless' of the recent past, maybe the spirit now is of a sharpening of the senses.

SHORTHAND

by Graham Meyer

'Shorthand' is a word in metamorphosis. It will soon go the way of 'milkman', 'corset', and 'riding shotgun', its literal meaning fluttering historically away, leaving only its connotational cocoon behind. 'Shorthand' will still be a shorthand for abbreviation, but shorthand itself won't be for anything. Shorthand's obsolescence is so obvious that an example sentence under 'stenography' in the online reference WordNet is 'Stenography is no longer a marketable skill'.

Before going to journalism school, I wanted to learn shorthand. It seemed useful for reporting, and it was wonderfully obscure to me. Its impending translation to the plane of the metaphorical only attracted me more.

I checked out a guide to learning the Gregg system from the university library. It was shelved on the bottom floor, where the stacks butt up face to face to save floorspace, then roll out when you need them—the shelves where items that deserve disposal and the buried treasures of the library coexist. Here, a squat book called *Analytical Lessons in Gregg Shorthand* was exactly where the computer catalog claimed. ('Card catalog' is another swansong word.) The date stamps on the inside-back-cover pouch showed a flurry of activity in the 1950s, then a flare-out. The last date stamped was in the 1970s.

I started running through the lessons and exercises. Gregg shorthand spells words phonetically, a simple stroke representing each sound. Similar sounds have similar strokes: 't' is a short upward slash, 'd' a longer one. Vowels are represented by loops. The stenographer only lifts the pen at the end of a word, except in cases of further abbreviation.

These further abbreviations frustrated me. The characters 'd' and 's' connected mean 'dear sir'. 'G' alone is 'goods'. 'Mk' is 'market'. They weren't intuitive to my 21st-century brain. They evoked heavily made-up women in flowery knee-length dresses scribbling for cigar-chewers.

I also found my handwriting unfit for shorthand. I write in small, jerky letterforms, and I both hold the pen and press it into the paper too hard. When Gregg called for me to distinguish a smooth curve from a straight line, it took fierce concentration, which made elegance impossible. My shorthand was ugly.

Worst of all, I wasn't patient enough to learn any speed. I practiced for a week or two, and at the end I could print out a full sentence in a quarter the time shorthand took me.

I did figure out how shorthand works and why it exists, which I misunderstood before starting my dabbling. I had thought that shorthand was a writing system, designed to record speech. It's not. It's a tool for the stenographer to generate a code to translate back into English, preferably immediately, before forgetting which word an ambiguous squiggle represents. It's a memory aid for one person to communicate with a future self, not for two people to communicate with each other.

There's something lonely and beautiful about that, just as there is about shorthand crossing the river. I hope to admire it in its glass case, even as it dissolves from my memory, too.

D as in DESIRE: Since Deleuze is considered to be, says Parnet, a philosopher of desire, so what is it? Deleuze starts by saying that 'it's not what people thought it was, even then. It was a big ambiguity and a big misunderstanding, or rather a little one.' However, he then addresses the question in great, and often moving detail. First, like most people in writing a book, they thought that they would say something new, specifically that people who wrote before them didn't understand what desire meant. So as philosophers, Deleuze with Guattari saw their task as that of proposing a new concept of desire. And concepts, despite what some people think, refer to things that are extremely simple and concrete. Deleuze emphasizes that one never desires something, someone, but rather always desires an aggregate (ensemble). Deleuze refers to Proust when he says that desire for a woman is not so much desire for the woman as for a paysage, a landscape, that is enveloped in this woman.

RIETVELD RECON-STRUCTIONS

by Ryan Gander

Cut to an empty cork-tiled room, Los Angeles. White text over scene for 5 seconds:

A CORK-TILED ROOM, L.A.
NOVEMBER 2006

Informal male voiceover (throughout):

> I am a strong believer in the inherent inspirational qualities that materials can hold
> over a maker. In my mind this is a kind of superstitious alchemy, somewhere between
> moondust and the intangible fabric of the emperor's new clothes. And I love it.

Cut to the entrance hall of the Jan van Eyck Academie, Maastricht. People wander to and fro, in and out of the shot.
White text over scene for 5 seconds:

AN ENTRANCE HALL, MAASTRICHT
SEPTEMBER 1999

> On arriving in The Netherlands in 1999 for postgraduate study I was greeted in the
> entrance space of the Jan van Eyck Academie by a huddle of chairs and tables made
> from untreated sawn timber. The area where these chairs congregated was used as a
> meeting place for participants. Bread would be broken, stories would be told, friends
> would be made and sexually transmitted diseases would be shared …

Quite unwittingly, this huddle of furniture became part of my life. It transpired that the chairs were made by a burly Dutch man called Huub, the technical advisor of the Academy's woodwork shop. Meanwhile, the bogus red cotton-covered foam blocks that acted as cushions—and which seemed to bastardise the principles of the chairs' obviously modernist design—were made by the Academy's secretary at home on her sewing machine. I grew fond of Huub during my stay there. He wasn't the most approachable of people, and many of my fellow participants found him really hard to work with. Thinking back now that might have had something to do with his hard-working-class-work-ethic. I guess if you take someone from Industry—as he was—and drop them in an over-funded art school with a pack of trans-global spoilt brats walking around with laptops and wearing designer specs, there's bound to be a bit of friction.

I got to know Huub through my interest in his Rietveld furniture. I found out he'd once had a mini production line making these tables and chairs, about fifteen years beforehand when he was first employed by the Academie. Fifty-five chairs and twenty side-tables to be exact. Pinned to the wall of his windowless box room office at the back of the workshop were a few black and white A3 photocopies of a very dated-looking plan for the furniture. We would sit there together, drinking coffee and talking about these plans, which he assured me were very rare, although he would never tell me how he came upon them. The day I left Maastricht to go and live in Amsterdam, I found an envelope pushed under the door of the bare studio I was about to leave which contained photocopies of the plans and a post-it note, which read 'Don't show anyone', stuck to the first page. Two weeks later, by chance I came across a newly-published book entitled *Rietveld Meubels om Zelf te Maken*—How to make Rietveld furniture—in the shop of the Stedelijk Museum with exactly the same plans in it. I soon discovered that the photocopies Huub had so preciously given me were from the 1986 second edition of that book. I initially felt a little deflated, but in retrospect I think Huub was trying to instill in my mind—or preserve in his own—some kind of uniqueness or exclusivity around the chairs, to curb their increasing popularity. At this point, however, the significance of that furniture for me had not quite yet been realised.

Cut to various shots of the streets of Utrecht, ending on the Rietveld-Schröder house, then details of furniture construction instructions. White text over scenes for first 5 seconds:

UTRECHT
MAY 1936

Gerrit Rietveld was born in Utrecht and stayed there all his life. His father was a cabinetmaker, and Gerrit started working in his shop at the age of twelve. By 1934 he was a qualified architect and making a lot of furniture. That year he designed a series of utilitarian furniture intended for the masses, produced by Metz & Co. of Amsterdam. This was during the depression, and the furniture was designed in direct response to the harsh economic climate of the early thirties. The pieces were made from cheap red spruce usually used for packing cases, and designed for self-assembly at home. The series was called 'Crate Furniture'. Being prone to exaggeration and embellishment, when relating this story I often tell people that the lengths of sawn timber are cut without waste from the exact dimensions of planks taken from cargo crates containing tea from the Dutch colony of Surinam. Who knows? ... No, really, I mean, *who* knows? I would love to hear this story confirmed. Rietveld proposed that 'a piece of furniture made of high-grade wood and manufactured completely according to traditional production methods is transported in a crate to avoid damage ... no

18

one has ever ascertained that such a chest embodies an improvised, highly purposeful method of carpentry … there must therefore at long last be someone who chooses the crate rather than the piece of furniture.' Unfortunately, I don't think the idea ever really quite caught on. Certainly the chairs weren't very popular at the time.

Cut to fast-forward video footage of Fred Evans (FE) building a chair in an artist's studio, London. White text over scenes for first 5 seconds:

AN ARTIST'S STUDIO, LONDON
NOVEMBER 2005

Fred Evans, aged six, accompanied by his mother Caroline, is invited to my studio, given twenty planks of sawn timber, the materials of a deconstructed Rietveld armchair, and told to make something. Fred strategically, or perhaps randomly, selects two pieces and positions them butted up against each other at a jaunty angle. I drill a hole, countersink and insert a screw to join pieces together for him. This process continues until all the pieces are used. This is an experiment that I have thought about doing for quite some time without really knowing why. Throughout Fred's work I am encouraging, but consciously attempting to censor myself from contributing creatively to the construction process.

I realise later that I wasn't really censoring myself enough, but enough for what? It isn't an experiment because I don't have a hypothesis to prove or disprove, nor any research methods from which to document results and draw conclusions. I remember this from GSCE science lessons. I also remember that one of the most important things in an experiment is the Control. To achieve reliable findings the conditions of the experiment must be identical each time the experiment is conducted. I find myself toying with the idea of repeating this exercise, ten times, to make the process more scientific. The thesis seems to be developing backwards. I note to myself that nothing must change apart from the subject—which I realise is the child, not the chair.

Cut to interior of the Rivington Grill, London. White text over scenes for first 5 seconds:

A BAR, LONDON
JUNE 2005

I am in a bar with Bedwyr Williams. Out of the blue we are joined by two artists from Glasgow called 'Blood and Feathers'. These are not their real names. Within thirty minutes an argument breaks out between myself and one of the Glaswegians. Actually she isn't Glaswegian, she's from Preston, but is implicated in the Glasgow art scene, which for the purposes of this vignette qualifies her as Glaswegian. Anyway, the argument is instigated by me making a slightly drunken, flippant remark about her work possessing a 'Glasgow aesthetic'. She is visibly offended and asks me to explain what the Glasgow aesthetic looks like. I start to squirm a bit as I realise I don't really know. I mean, I know what I'm talking about looks like, but I can't articulate it very well. In a way I'm arguing for the sake of arguing, as is common when drunk, but I realise I'm a little angrier than I should reasonably be. To try to prevent myself looking like a complete idiot, and probably achieving the opposite, I use the term 'Faux Modernism' and describe that idea as looking like something to do with a pimped-up Kraftwerk album cover or the jottings and scribblings on a sixth-form Goth's backpack. Some days later, in the middle of an email discussion with Stuart in relation to my fictional word 'Mitim', I find myself repeating this 'Faux Modernism' idea that I so inadequately in the bar. I resolve to spend some time having a think about it before I open my big mouth again.

Cut to repeat of previous fast-forward video footage of FE building a chair in the London studio. White text over scenes for first 5 seconds:

AN ARTIST'S STUDIO, LONDON
NOVEMBER 2005

In truth, Fred Evans, aged six, accompanied by his mother Caroline, paid two visits to my studio. The first was not too dissimilar to the way I described it previously, but there are notable discrepancies. Fred actually began to assemble the pieces given to him in a very ordered and considered manner. At some point during the process, to my horror the object he was making started to resemble a box, and slowly as time passed as piece by piece was added it became apparent that he was, in fact, the son of Sol LeWitt. He was making a perfect cube, the little bastard!

That cube was undoubtedly the most flawless part of the whole project, but obviously I wasn't after flawlessness. At this point I felt that the experiment hadn't really yet begun and the conditions weren't exactly in place. As it happened, Fred started to get a little aggravated too, perhaps partly brought on by the sugar in the tube of Smarties and Lemonade I had on offer. The object he was making didn't have the jaunty angles and protruding struts I had expected from a six-year-old let loose with these materials, and although I feel quite bad about it now, I had the idea that both Fred and his mum Caroline could sense my bewilderment and surprise, which they may have confused with disappointment, which led to the decision by all parties involved that the partially-constructed sculpture should be disassembled and the process recommenced afresh the following week. I feel quite accountable for this. If Fred had been left to his own devices we would probably be looking at an interesting anomaly rather than the pleasingly abstract contraption that was produced by him on his following visit. My guilt is bubbling away here. Still … one-nil to me.

Cut to a kitchen table, Scarborough Street, London. White text over scene for first 5 seconds:

I spent a bit of time thinking about the 'Faux-Modernist' thing some more after Stuart yelled at me and told me I really should get my story straight before writing anything down. And I came up with this:

There's a lot of art and design around at the moment that uses an appropriated modernist aesthetic. Traditionally, we think of the modernist aesthetic as borne from ethics, or at least an explicit set of values, function above form, et cetera. So how does that translate into the idea of an artwork that exudes these values but is not necessarily produced under them? This work surely becomes purely emblematic; something that visually or iconically reminds us of a set of values because it looks like another thing originally made by that yardstick. There is an obvious difference between simply referencing modernist form—keying into a history—and actually working under its values, and I guess I was getting upset about the ubiquity of the former.

But what about my non-experiment? There's indeed part of me that wants to make a 'modernist-looking' sculpture which is 'easy', both physically and aesthetically—and I'm sure I could make a really convincing one and that I'd really enjoy making it. But it's problematic. Since the mid-nineties that modernist look is an easy art world currency which I increasingly find myself criticising, like in the pub. In effect I'm cancelling myself out of the possibility of doing it myself, or at the very least setting myself up for a bout of self-loathing, which I can do without. I realise, then, that asking Fred to assist me in this process is actually is a some subconscious counter-process I'm setting up to achieve a clone of what I wish to critique—or maybe *highlight* is a better word, without actually making it myself, but still enjoying the creation. Making it one step removed, then, and conceptually it works like child's play. My undercover idea was that all the sculptures made by the children would appear—to any spectator unaware of the conditions under which they had been made—to be a generic sculpture made by an artist now, at this time, in this city, London, in this epoch that will come to be known in the future as the era of 'Faux Modernism'.

I want to be part of it so as not to be part of it. My hypothesis had formed. I will make ten sculptures with ten children, each from a single deconstructed Rietveld cargo chair. I expect that the majority will be functionless, abstract, chaotic forms reminiscent of a stereotypical constructivist or modernist aesthetic. There are two important points to consider: one, the makers have no knowledge of modernist ethics, values or principles; and two, the material—wood—previously constituted modernist ethics, values or principles.

If the hypothesis was proved correct, I decided, it would be for one of these two reasons: one, children are inherently inclined to make something that approximates the modernist aesthetics described previously, i.e., *their naivety matches that of modernism*; or two, the essence or spirit of modernism is transferred through materials, i.e., *has somehow got into the wood.* I hadn't—and haven't—yet worked out how to divide the two. That's for a later experiment. Anyway, with this hypothesis in mind I decide to make nine more sculptures under the same conditions.

Cut to same London studio as before. Video footage of a RIETVELD RECONSTRUCTION (2006). White text over scenes for first 5 seconds:

I'm being advised by Rose, the younger sister of my girlfriend. It's the first time I've met her, and I'm a bit distracted from the work in hand because of the significance of the social situation. When it's over, we're off to the Hard Rock Café on Park Lane for a burger and a milkshake, followed by a drive to the Suffolk countryside to take Rose home. You might say I'm seeing things through Rose-tinted spectacles. In fact, the making of this sculpture has pretty much escaped my memory, but looking back at the pictures, it seemed to be a hybrid of order and chaos, a sort of systematic muddle. The object was made in two halves, I remember that. The first section was a cross laid on the floor, and I think we talked about it being a bit like a canal system, and the second half which we later joined to the first part was more like an incomplete cube. I do remember a sheet of holographic acid-house smiley stickers were on a table in my studio for some reason, and I passed them to Rose to see if she wanted them. Rose stuck one onto the sculpture to brand it. I remember thinking that I'd ruined the experiment again, because I'd not stuck to the control conditions. Shortly after, I also wondered if I should've been using the word 'sculpture' when talking with her about it. After all doesn't 'sculpture' already suggest something abstract or alien-looking? Something non-functional, decorative, which again messes up the supposedly neutral conditions.

Cut to interior of an Amsterdam art gallery. Video footage of a RIETVELD RECONSTRUCTION (2006). White text over scenes for first 5 seconds:

A GALLERY, AMSTERDAM
JUNE 2006

I am working in the gallery with my gallerist's son, Abel, on a sculpture which will be exhibited in the show as soon as it is made. He is seven years old and knows it. He is an extraordinary child, in fact there's something prodigal about him. He is by far the most coy and hesitant of all the kids, but also the most astute, and he works very, very fast. The thing he makes does, actually, in all honesty, look very much like Tatlin's Tower, yet built in the most illogical way. For a start he builds it lying down, and only right at the end stands it up. He explains to me where the cars should park underneath, and how the lifts go up and down the sides and where people can enter and exit. It isn't at all abstract to him, but it's not logical or considered either. Although it immediately appears abstract to a stranger, he has obviously made clear sense of the abstraction. It is the most beautiful so far, by quite some way, though I still can't really fathom why. Perhaps it's something to do with the fact that while it appears abstract, there's a certain familiarity to the angles, mass, line, form and weight, so it's not uncomfortably spastic. Its form lies well within the psyche, but very latent and subconscious. This suddenly seems somewhere beyond that simple emblem referencing modernist history. At this point I feel I might actually be learning something.

Cut to interior of a Bologna art gallery. Video footage of a RIETVELD RECONSTRUCTION (2006). White text over scenes for first 5 seconds:

A GALLERY, BOLOGNA
APRIL 2006

In Italy I'm making a Rietveld reconstruction with Diego, the grandson of the caretaker of the pavilion where the show is. We are working in the living space of Le Corbusier's Esprit Nouveau Pavilion, presented to the City of Bologna by the City of Paris. The original building was realised as an ephemeral pavilion for the Paris Universal Expo in 1925 and rebuilt more than fifty years later in 1977 in the middle of Bologna Fair District. Diego is given the parts that would usually make up two chairs and one side table. Again, not exactly under the precise conditions I spoke about before, I know, but I'm caring less and less about the control. The energy and excitement I get from the act of making these sculptures is increasingly substituting any need for analytical results. My subject this time is a boisterous Italian nine-year-old who naturally doesn't speak any English. The sculpture is made with the help of a translator. He quickly gets to work and, again to my surprise, constructs a gigantic tower, constructed in three separate parts that I am directed to stack one on top of each other and fix together. The idea that this is assembled from three separate components is an oddity, but I'm intrigued. I can't help but think that somehow he was aware of the fact that the singular pile of wooden planks he was given was derived from three separate entities. The outcome is therefore in line with my materials theory.

Cut to interior of a London art fair. Video footage of a RIETVELD RECONSTRUCTION (2006). White text over scenes for first 5 seconds:

AN ART FAIR, LONDON
OCTOBER 2006

This situation feels like a pressure cooker. It's the opening of the Frieze Art Fair in London, and what started as a simple exercise has unnecessarily evolved into a spectacle. There is a large audience, as well as sundry photographers and a BBC film crew. In addition, it turns out that Santa's little helper this time is not one child, but two. I feel very awkward and uncomfortable in this situation, and begin to question whether I am making these poor kids perform like dancing bears. I certainly feel like I'm dancing myself. To ease the situation I suggest to the kids' mother that the work should be carried out by just one of the sisters, rather than both of them—namely the eldest, again called Rose. This is translated into Dutch to the two girls standing patiently in front of the pile of wood. Word by word I witness the youngest girl's face slowly drop from a beaming smile to one of disappointment. Then I see her eyes well up with tears, and she starts blinking fast trying so as not to cry, in an attempt to be grown-up for the crowd. A minute later she is bawling uncontrollably in her mother's arms. I feel like the audience are all looking at me, frowning and tutting, accompanied by mutterings from the crowd. 'Oh why doesn't he make it with them both?', 'Poor kid, she really wanted to do it …' I feel like a Bad Guy. It's terrible, so I rapidly go back on my decision and hold out a piece of wood at arms length, beckoning the youngest to join in, and they're soon both at work. It's by far the quickest sculpture to date due to the gruelling situation. The result is as anticipated this time: a beautiful monster.

Cut to same London studio as before. Video footage of mystery book bags and a RIETVELD RECONSTRUCTION (2006). White text over scenes for first 5 seconds:

AN ARTIST'S STUDIO, LONDON
MARCH 2006

At this point I had a new idea. I realised it was a bit late into the process to be changing things, but I had recently found eight bags of second-hand books at my local library on Camomile Street and I made the decision to add one of these bags to each sculpture— a white plastic carrier bag with a City of London crest and the name of the library. The tops of the bags have been sealed with packaging tape, so it's impossible for the purchaser to see what titles are. On the front of the bag there is a sticker that reads 'Mystery bag, a bag full of PBK's for two pounds, Adventure Category, please pay at the enquiry desk with correct change, thank you'. I secured an Adventure bag, two Romance bags, one Biography, one Science Fiction, one Travel, one Children's and one Crime. They were perfect. The instructions to the child were simple: the bag couldn't be opened but had to sit with the object when it was finished. By now you're probably frowning and confused. My reasoning for adding the bags was that if all the sculptures did all happen to end up the same, the bags would act as some sort of red-herring—for the child, the spectator, and myself. For the child in so far as acting as some form of obscure inspiration, for the spectator as a distraction, and to give me something new to look at and think about over the course of the following eight.

Cut to same London studio as before. Video footage of a RIETVELD RECONSTRUCTION (2006) :

My friend Adam comes to the studio around lunchtime with his son Cosimo. Adam is an Art Insurer, involved in shipping, galleries and storage, which gets me thinking that Cosimo has probably seen a lot of art already in his short life. I guess he knows what it is supposed to look like. This is another flaw in the master-plan. It didn't occur to me until about the sixth sculpture that all the parents whose children I'd asked to borrow were, in fact, artists, gallerists or otherwise associated with the art world in some other way. I am evidently not a very consistent scientist. Anyway, Cosimo produced a beautiful abstract … thing, so I give him enough money to buy the complete *Star Wars* series on DVD. He told me he'd never seen any of them, and I found this so astonishing that I wanted to make sure he saw them in the correct order. He placed his bag of Romance next to the sculpture and I sent him on his way.

Cut to same London studio as before. Video footage of 2 more completed RIETVELD RECONSTRUCTIONS. White text over scenes for first 5 seconds:

ALEX AND TOM (SORRY)
THE SAME THING, SOME PLACE,
SOME TIME

There's a certain amount of fiction in my work. It's something I'm interested in and it's something that I manage to deal with, morally and ethically, because I'm making art which is not about *The Real*. It's about making conditions for other possibilities to exist … or so I keep telling myself. I have produced milestones from broken concrete from a Le Corbusier building in Marseilles that was really made by my dad in his garage in north Wales with B&Q cement mix. I have made a photograph of my family before me titled MY FAMILY BEFORE ME that wasn't actually taken before I was born—I just wasn't there because I was in hospital. And I've had a crossword published in *The Times* containing a fictional word I invented, only it was really a single forged sheet printed with the same technique and wrapped around the real paper of that day. This is the nature of the production of conceptual art: the by-products are merely there to carry the idea.

Do you ever think Cornelia Parker really sent that meteorite that landed in her garden back to space with NASA? Ever seen a photo or a letter? I doubt it, but right now, as you're reading this there are maybe three or four people somewhere in the world sitting around a bar room table saying, 'Did you hear about the artist who sent a meteorite back to space …' But that's not the really strange thing. The *really* strange thing is someone else somewhere else is also talking about it *now*! … and someone else *now*! *That* is the work, and it wouldn't make it less of a thing if it never even existed in the first place, right? Sounds like I'm convincing myself, I know. Perhaps I am.

I have another confession to make. Two of the children in the Rietveld experiment were fictional too. Even typing this now turns my stomach and fills me with dread because one of those sculptures by a fictional child was sold to a good friend of mine and I never told him. I think if I did tell him he probably wouldn't mind, but I don't feel the need to find out right now. The thing is, of course if I'm going to harp on about ethics and aesthetics, if I'm going to talk about values, then I should come clean and also admit that there was no conceptual reason for me to make two of the sculptures as if I were a young kid. The first one was made after a night of heavy drinking. I returned to my studio, where I was living at the time, and under the pressure of a gallery I faked one that was to due to be collected by FedEx the next morning. Bad man. The second was a quick-fix situation due to a child not turning up to produce the work at an opening. In the panic I constructed something in fifteen minutes around the back of the conference centre by a fire escape near the bins, so as to not be rumbled by the other galleries. These aren't even good reasons are they? Sorry Tom, sorry Alex.

Cut to interior of an Amsterdam gallery. Video footage of a RIETVELD RECONSTRUCTION (2006). White text over scenes for first 5 seconds:

25

A GALLERY, AMSTERDAM
JUNE 2006

A slightly shy but quite mature Dutch boy called, appropriately enough, Beer, began the construction process slowly and thoughtfully. Six people were present at the construction of the sculpture. Myself, actively helping to build the work and, then at some distance in the same room, his mother—the gallerist—and three other gallery staff. Beer spoke some English, which was good as my Dutch is atrocious, though I tried to make an effort by muttering lines from television commercials that had been drummed into me, to make him laugh: *Red Bull geeft je vleugels!*

I'm not aware at what point exactly young Beer made a choice between form and function, but there most definitely was a point that everyone in the gallery acknowledged. The sculpture started as the others did, haphazard, free and without objective, but as the object took form, silence fell across the gallery and glances were exchanged. No one spoke for superstition that it would ruin what was happening, but we all simultaneously moved closer and closer in, forming a small pocket watching wide-eyed as Beer reconstructed a deconstructed Rietveld chair back into a Rietveld chair.

I think I broke the silence first, but managed to wait until there were only three more planks remaining. 'He's gone and made a Rietveld!' Of course the chair was not a precise replica—it was short of a few pieces because a small desk had been made too—but the resemblance was unmistakable. Even the incline of the back mimicked the angle of the original. I asked Beer's mother if he had ever seen a real Rietveld chair, or whether she knew if they had been taught about Rietveld in school. She was pretty certain he hadn't. On completion, Beer tried out his newfound workstation, and as he sat there proudly it crossed my mind that the look on that innocent child's face was not exactly one of pride, but instead of smugness—smugness for cheating me! I began to hate him and his stupid fucking chair and in a moment of paranoia I began to wonder whether he had been tipped off, and who exactly had put him up to it.

Cut to same London studio as before, now empty. White text over scenes for first 5 seconds:

AN ARTIST'S STUDIO, LONDON
JANUARY 2007

A few weeks ago I read an article in the *NME* I really liked about some unknown band from Yorkshire. At some point the writer suggested that 'northern folk model themselves on the things they hate rather than the things they like'. Apart from it being ridiculously stereotypical and although this statement suggests that we northern folk come with an inherent air of negativity and bitterness, I do like the idea of evolving as a person knowing what you definitely don't want to be, rather than wanting to be like something else. That way you don't know where you are going, so it's much easier to get lost, like with this 'Faux-Modernist' chip I'm carrying around on my shoulder. By now I've become happily resigned to my so-called experiment. As such, it wasn't a very good idea to start with, and if I'd have proved my thesis, so what? I could start all over again, try harder, not intervene, keep control, and refuse to be swayed by external pressures … but in the end the ethics just aren't there.

Cut to shot through a car windscreen driving through Los Angeles. White text over scene for first 5 seconds:

SOME WHERE, SOME PLACE,
IN THE FUTURE

So far I've only made nine of the ten sculptures, but I have a new mate called Arlo, who is four. We get on quite well although he hits me a lot. I still need to ask, but I'm hoping he'll agree to be subject ten. If so, maybe he'll be the one I leave to his own devices.

as in ENFANCE (CHILDHOOD): Deleuze refers to someone recounting seeing a horse die in the street before the age of the automobile, and he translates this into the task of becoming a writer: Deleuze cites Dostoyevski, the dancer Nijinksi, Nietzsche, all of whom witnessed a horse dying in the street. But Deleuze insists, 'I was a child,' and the importance of this indefinite article is the multiplicity of a child.

as in FIDELITY: Finally, Deleuze says that all people only have charm through their madness [folie]. What is charming is the side of someone that shows that they're a bit unhinged [où ils perdent un peu les pédales]. If you can't grasp the small trace of madness in someone, you can't be their friend. But if you grasp that small point of insanity, 'démence,' of someone, the point where they are afraid or even happy, that point of madness is the very source of his/her charm. The indefinite article has an extreme richness. He then pauses, smiles, and says: 'D'où 'G' [Which leads us to 'G'] …

as in GAUCHE (LEFT): Parnet asks Deleuze if he had becomings-revolutionary himself at that moment, and he says that her smile tells him it's a question not devoid of mockery. So she rephrases it: Between Deleuze's cynicism as a 'homme de gauche'/ leftist and his becoming-revolutionary as a leftist, how does he unravel, explain all that [se débrouiller', and what does it mean for Deleuze to be 'de gauche', on the left? Deleuze pauses here before answering. Then he says he does not believe that a leftist government exists, which is not astonishing. The best one can hope for, he believes, is a government favorable to certain demands from the left. So how to define being on the left, he continues? In two ways: first, it's a matter of perception, which means this: what would NOT being on the left mean? It's a little like an address, extending outward from a person: the street where you are, the city, the country, other countries farther and farther away [Deleuze gestures outward]. It starts from the self, and to the extent that one is privileged, living in a rich country, one might ask, what can we do to make this situation last? Being on the left is the opposite: it's perceiving … And people say the Japanese perceive like that, not like us … they perceive first the periphery [Deleuze gestures outward inward], they would say the world, the continent—let's say Europe —France, etc. etc., rue de Bizerte, me: it's a phenomenon of perception, perceiving the horizon, perceiving on the horizon.

27

H

as in HISTORY OF PHILOSOPHY: So, it's not that he is particularly modest, Deleuze says, but it strikes him as being quite shocking were there philosophers who simply said, hey, I'm going into philosophy now, going to do my own philosophy. These are feeble statements, argues Deleuze, because philosophy is like [painting with] colors, before entering into it, one has to take so many precautions, before conquering the 'philosophical color' [la couleur philosophique]—and the philosophical color is the concept. Before succeeding in inventing concepts, an enormous amount of work is necessary. Deleuze sees the history of philosophy as this slow modesty, taking a long time doing portraits. It's like a novelist, Deleuze suggests, who might say, I'm writing novels, but cannot read any because I'd risk compromising my inspiration. Deleuze says he has heard young writers make such frightening statements which, for him, means they simply do not need to work. At this point, it becomes a bit mysterious, says Deleuze, and he asks Parnet perhaps to give him another question so he can define this.

I

as in IDEA: Parnet begins by saying that this 'idea' is no longer in the Platonic domain. Rather, she says, Deleuze always spoke passionately about philosophers' ideas, but also ideas of thinkers in cinema (directors), artists' and painters' ideas. He always preferred an 'idea' to explications and commentary. So why, for Deleuze, does the 'idea' take precedence over everything else? Deleuze admits that this is quite correct: the 'idea' as he uses it traverses all creative activities, since creating means having an idea. But there are people —not at all to be scorned for this—who go through life without ever having an idea. Deleuze insists that it is usually quite rare to have an idea, it doesn't happen every day. And a painter is no less likely to have ideas than a philosopher, just not the same kind of ideas.

J

as in JOY: Deleuze says [with some laughter from Parnet in response] that if he hadn't been a philosopher and if he had been a woman, he would have wanted to be a wailer [pleureuse], the complaint rises and it's an art. And the complaint has this perfidious side as well, as if to say: don't take on my complaint, don't touch me, don't feel sorry for me, I'm taking care of it. And in taking care of it for oneself, the complaint is transformed: what is happening is too overwhelming for me, because this is joy, joy in a pure state. The complaint is not only joy, it's also unease, because, in fact, realizing a force can require a price: one wonders, am I going to risk my skin/life [laisser ma peau]?

K

as in KANT: What does Kant do? Parenthetically, Deleuze reminds Parnet that all he is doing here is constantly to consider what it means to create a concept. Continuing, he says Kant creates a concept because he reverses the subordination, so that with him, movement depends on time. And suddenly, time changes its nature, it ceases being circular. Before, time is subordinate to movement in which movement is the great periodic movement of heavenly bodies, so it's circular. On the contrary, when time is freed from movement and movement depends on time, then time becomes a straight line. Deleuze recalls something Borges said— although he has little relation to Kant—that a more frightening labyrinth than a circular labyrinth is one in a straight line, marvelous, but it was Kant who lets time loose.

HITCHCOCK

Have you ever seen an assembly line?

TRUFFAUT

No, I never have.

HITCHCOCK

They're absolutely fantastic. I wanted to
have a long dialogue scene between Cary
Grant and one of the factory workers as
they walk along the assembly line. They
might, for instance, be talking about one
of the foremen. Behind them a car is being
assembled, piece by piece. Finally, the
car they've seen being put together from
a simple nut and bolt is complete, with
gas and oil, and all ready to drive off
the line. The two men look at it and say,
'Isn't it wonderful?' Then they open
the door to the car and out drops a corpse!

TRUFFAUT

That's a great idea!

HITCHCOCK

Where has the body come from? Not from the
car, obviously, since they've seen it start
at zero! The corpse falls out of nowhere,
you see! And the body might be that of
the foreman the two fellows have been
discussing.

TRUFFAUT

That's a perfect example of absolute
nothingness! Why did you drop the idea?
Is it because it would have made the scene
too long?

HITCHCOCK

It wasn't a question of time. The real
problem was that we couldn't integrate
the idea into the story. Even a gratuitous
scene must have some justification for
being there, you know![1]

MODERN TIMES

by Melissa Gronlund

Anthropomorphic automata, the endlessness of the assembly line, the repetition of gestures that turns into humans into machines—all these lie behind the idea of the uncanny that Freud identified as endemic to modernity, and central to the anxious aesthetics of Modernism. In Hitchcock's hands, this malice would have been linked, as ever, to the forward-moving build-up of suspense, figured literally in the film by the assembly line.

The curator of this summer's Documenta, Roger M. Buergel, has made the question, 'Is modernity our antiquity?', one of his key themes, publishing a book on the subject in advance of the exhibition. The question was actually first posed by T. J. Clark in 1999, when the art historian asked whether modern*ism* was our antiquity. The tell-tale switching of the suffixes—'-ism' to '-ity'—suggests a shift from a question that begs answers of an art-historical nature to one that casts its glance wider into the social facts of modernity. Not only artists, but society in general has difficulty recognising a past before modernity: the clip-clop of carriages and hand-sewn clothes appear irrevocably distant. And is that modernity—automobiles and store-bought outfits? The facts are getting lost in the -isms. Perhaps another way into the question about modernity and antiquity is to look at the objects themselves that constitute modernity, and which led, apparently, to Modernism, to the shock of the new and the break with the past: trains, the telephone, the typewriter; factories, industrial complexes, vast public transport systems; electric lighting, electric toothbrushes, dishwashers, vacuum cleaners, portable music devices. Modernism sought to incorporate these objects and the new landscape of secular, atomised modern life into some kind of order —an order that represented utopian possibilities for a better social environment. It is when coupled with this promise of real-life improvement that Modernism trades its adjectival status and achieves its capital letter 'M'.

Hitchcock's proposed scenario was not explicitly Modernist, but the subject matter and its implications address the anxieties of industrialisation as succinctly as Fritz Lang's *Metropolis* (1927) does. Cinematic represent-ations of factories, in fact, consistently strike a low note of dread. Factories figure as sites of the uncanny: locales of psychosexual violence and pathology where menace and agitation spill out into the seedy, aberrant behaviour of its workers. Gene Wilder plays Willy Wonka as a fey man with a soft spot for young children; he shuts himself in with his factory, staffed by squat human mon-strosities and cooks up an elaborate moral quest with his factory as the fetishised, almost Pyrrhic prize. In Tim Burton's version, Wonka's pathology is rounded out by childhood trauma, and set in thick pale foundation spackled onto Johnny Depp's primed pearly skin. The heights of violence reached by both films—the programmatic murder of each child—is as extraordinary as the film's ability to pan the guilt off into the mechanised process and products of the factory. Willy Wonka doesn't ever seem terribly reprehensible.

Steven Soderbergh made his murder mystery *Bubble* (2005), which takes place in a doll factory, in a realist aesthetic and, in a sense, ethic—he shot it cheaply on digital, used amateur rather than professional actors, and bypassed the Hollywood release schedule of a blockbuster opening weekend for a multi-format release in cinemas and DVDs on the same day. While the film itself is uneven, the actors' lack of affect is mesmerising; no one seems completely aware of how their actions will appear, and they err conservatively on the side of detachment. Soderbergh exploits the workplace: the disembodied body parts that wait incorporation in the factory, the workers' task of spray-painting faces on plastic heads, the transformation of flesh-coloured plastic into overdone, prepubescent showgirls. The central character is Kyle, a twenty-something stoner, who at the beginning of the film is looked after by Martha, an irritable co-worker whose maternal solicitude for Kyle is just a heartbeats short of quickening desire. Kyle is murdered after an argument one night, and the whodunnit begins to unfold, eventually revealing Martha as the culprit —the older woman, punished for her unnatural, unrequited lust for the younger man.

Rather than symbolising psychosexual abnormality, the films suggest factories as the cause of this abnormality: the constant repetition, the self-containment and claustrophobia of the factory world, the hierarchical structure of boss and workers. The interminability of the assembly line is repeatedly emphasised, either in positive —i.e., the boredom of the workers in *Bubble*— or in negative, through conspicuous disruption. The bizarrely cast Björk and Catherine Deneuve break out into song in the factory musical *Dancer in the Dark* (2000); Laverne and Shirley, in the famous opening credits to their TV show, place a glove on the line of beer bottles they're meant to be capping, signalling out the individual bottle from the mass. The assembly line's unfolding perspective dominates: factories are rarely shown, as they were in Charlie Chaplin's *Modern Times* (1936) or Alexander Medvedkin's *Happiness* (1935), in long-shot. The point of view tends to be tied to a character and the factory apparatus unfolds bit by bit, with the knowledge of the whole out of reach.

The self-reflexivity contrived by Tacita Dean in her recent film *Kodak* (2006), in which she recorded the closing of the last double-sprocketed Super 16-mm film factory in France on the last five rolls of stock it produced, came naturally to early modern film, as in *Modern Times* or *Happiness*. When they showed elements of modernity—trains, trams, telephone and telegram wires, factories— on film, the spectacle of novelty, and fears they carried, accrued to each in unforced symmetry. The fact that modernity and Modernism are separate entities has become a truism.

Near the end of the interview that Truffaut conducted with Hitchcock, the normally reticent director discusses another failed possibility, a city symphony film that would follow 24 hours in the life of San Francisco, beginning with the food arriving across the urban landscape, meals being prepared, eaten and eventually sewage dumped into the ocean (he said the 'theme might be the rottenness of humanity'). Hitchcock searched for a plot to hang the film around but came up with nothing, and realised the scale of the picture would be too big for the audience to appreciate any of it. 'The tragedy is that the public accepts modernity without being awed by it.'[2]

The question of modernity being our antiquity gives a narrative to the past century: there was the past, of modernity and Modernism, and there is the present. The contemporary reuse of Modernist styles is then ironic, or knowing, or done by pastiche, and the facts of modernity are historic, and no longer current to us now. Perhaps we could look back to alternate

perceptions of time: two different notions co-exist in the Bible, for instance—one of them linear, and one of them called kairotic, or eternal time, which means that certain events recur regularly to prove that God encompasses past, present and eternity. Consider how beautiful that word is—the high optimism of kai and the earthy innuendo of eros that closes the sound, *kai...rotic*—and think of modernity that way. Is it so far away as to be antique, in the way that the Greco-Roman period was the antiquity of 19th-century classicism? What about its ambition, and its grounding in a life that is still startling—full of jagged edges that we have not yet absorbed, or the kind of love that makes pop songs seem profound. Modernity has not passed yet, and its circling modernisms continue to accompany it like restless fireflies. If factories continue to frighten us, can modernity be so far in the past?

NOTES
1. François Truffaut, *Hitchcock* (New York: Simon & Schuster, 1983), p.257. Though Hitchcock was not able to fit his proposed factory sequence into the finished film, Steven Spielberg pays homage to it in *Minority Report* which, like *North by Northwest*, is a story-board of iconic sequences; Hitchcock's original, Spielberg's quoted.
2. Hitchcock, quoted in Truffaut, ibid., p.320.

as in LITERATURE: So the question Parnet raises, Deleuze says, is quite sound, but he argues that one should not believe that, without experience, one can judge what is being created. What Deleuze prefers and what brings him great joy is when something that he is creating off on his own has an echo in a young painter's or a young writer's work. In that way, Deleuze feels that he can have a kind of encounter with what is happening currently, with another mode of creation. Parnet says that painting and cinema, for example, are favored for such encounters since he goes to galleries and to the movies, but that she has trouble imagining him strolling into a bookstore. Deleuze says she's right, that literature is so corrupted by the system of distribution, of literary prizes, that it's not even worth the trouble.

PRIVATE LANGUAGE

by Graham Meyer

Ludwig Wittgenstein, in *Philosophical Investigations*, says private language is impossible. Part of his argument depends on what he means by a private language—he doesn't mean just writing in a diary that no one else sees, or coining one's own words, or scrawls of shorthand that no one else can decipher. He's talking about a system of signs and referents that can't possibly be translated for another to understand. A code to represent private realities that no one else can access. 'I feel flooper today', the milkman said to himself.

Wittgenstein says the second time the sign is used, there's no way to verify that usage is consistent. Either we appeal to the private linguist's own impression of correctness, which is like asking someone whether she thinks she's honest, or we must assume there was a real connection between the sign and the referent originally, a connection being faithfully replicated here. To prove the private language, we're trying to prove there's a sign-referent connection, and we have to assume it in order to prove it. 'As if someone were to buy several copies of the morning paper to assure himself that what it said was true', Wittgenstein says. Appropriately enough, the argument, like the communication, is circular.

Language, though, is not just a lexicon linking signs to referents. In the concatenation of words comes style, history, beauty. All these qualities also carry information. Wittgenstein's vision of language is a bare room, shelter enough for meaning, but without creature comforts. Each of us has a private language with its own quirks and hidden poetry. The way you read the newspaper. The way you figure out a math problem. The way you know what she's going to say next.

Private language isn't a faithfully followed correspondence of signs to referents—it's the nub of the truth of individuality. Consistency is irrelevant. Only the rightness of the word in the moment matters, even if it's for the nonce. Why must a language be justified by testing its consistency? Would we demand Schiller write 'Ode to Joy' over again to make sure the subject of the poem was consistent from one time to the next?

Our experience of our own consciousness makes Wittgenstein's project look small. Searching for exactitude in the pairing of any words with their private referents is superimposing a grid on a landscape, or sorting shore rocks by size. Wittgenstein's search shows us only that we can't have a word-referent matrix that's both out of reach of others and internally consistent.

Sure, it's true. But what is it compared with the spinning, sprouting, skidding cascade projected on your eyelids, perched off-balance between waking and sleeping, as your mind unspools ahead of you, telling you what you know to be true, until you open your eyes and it all vanishes into the gloom of your bedroom ceiling?

M

as in MALADY: Parnet says that, to finish up, she wants to ask about his projects, like the one on literature or 'What Is Philosophy?'. When he undertakes a project like these, what does he find enjoyable as an old man taking these on? She reminds him that earlier he said that perhaps he won't finish them, but that there is something amusing in them. Deleuze says that it's something quite marvelous, a whole evolution, and when one is old, one has a certain idea of what one hopes to do that becomes increasingly pure, more and more purified. Deleuze says he conceives of the famous Japanese line drawings, lines that are so pure and then there is nothing, nothing but little lines. That's how he conceives of an old man's project, something that would be so pure, so nothing, and at the same time, everything, marvelous. He means this as reaching a sobriety, something that can only come late in life. He points to 'What is Philosophy?', his research on it: first, it's quite enjoyable [très gai] at his age to feel like he knows the answer, and like he's the only one to know, as if he got on a bus, and nobody else there could know. [Parnet laughs] All of this, for Deleuze, is very enjoyable.

further from the truth: the wariness towards the psychological effects of transit gradually became displaced. The idea of being home in comfortable surroundings (of one's own making) eased an alienated mental sense of self, yet became counter-balanced by the physical side-effects of the inverse relation-ship between distance and time spent in the air. Taking off and touching down at the same time, the following day, after twelve hours' flight, came to a sum total of havoc with our friend's internal system. As always, the short trip by train was accompanied by a growing hunger, a dry mouth and a sense of total mental and physical emptiness, at odds with the state of completion related to being home.

Unlocking the blue gate at the side of the house, he walked through the ivy-covered brick arch, and down the red brick passage beside his house in order to pass through the garden and enter through the small kitchen at the back. Having been removed from his usual subconscious subroutines, after such a long period of absence, the minor imperfections that he usually took in the stride of his life became more apparent than usual, as though all banal habits were now worthy of mental notes. He had the usual trouble with the key in the rusted lock of the kitchen door, and insisted that he should phone the landlord in the morning, and put it to rights, once and for all. How could he have overlooked such an annoyance, all this time?

Realising that it was morning, even if his stomach told him it was supper-time, he was reminded of the approaching dilemma: sleep now and suffer later, or stay awake in heightened suffering of the chores of day, in order to sleep at the end of it, from true exhaustion. Having very little self-discipline, and knowing it too, our friend realised he had already given in even before he unlocked the door, pushed aside all mental notes, and set his will upon sleep.

Blinded by this new-found conviction, he stepped into the kitchen and overlooked the clean surfaces, the few items of washing up left drying, and the faded ink on the green note on the fridge saying "I Love You". Not wishing to waste energy by really looking, he assumed that the fridge was as empty as his stomach, and the option of going back outside to buy breakfast didn't even cross his mind at this point. Driven further into the interior of his home by the mental image of sleep, directly behind the wall to his left, and striding diagonally across the living room, dropping his bags on the way, out one door and in through another, straight into the bedroom, his momentum carried him with the slightest fall onto the waist-high bed. Rather than get up again to close the curtains, he attempted to hide from the daylight (which supposedly would keep him awake) by crawling under the duvet, removing his clothes there and dropping them item by item next to the bed. As with the take-off in the plane, he had no consciousness of 'falling' asleep, he simply slept, as was his wont.

Our friend says that from that sleep he awoke once more, and afterwards went through such surprising adventures that he

thinks that they should be told to our
friends, and indeed the public in general,
and therefore he proposes to tell them now.
But, he says, I think it would be better if I
told them in the first person, as if it were
myself who had gone through them; which,
indeed, will be the easier and more natural
to me, since I understand the feeling and
desires of the friend of whom I am telling
better than any one else in the world does.

CHAPTER 4

CHILDREN ALONG THE WAY

How long I had been sleeping became
steadily unclear to me. One time I awoke
when the light seemed to be more filtered,
the next time it was bright again, the next
time I opened my eyes it was dark. By this
changing light of the sun, I had a sense of
time passing, but the next times I fell asleep
and awoke again, the light became constant, more diffused, and grey, like the light

of a hazy day through frosted glass. I was increasingly occupied in regurgitating the conversation at the dinner table, yet could not tell whether my own thoughts on the subject were lucid or whether I should dismiss them as the effects of the temporal upset. How often had the most compelling problems seemed to have been unravelled and presented to me, clear as day, in this state of early-morning slumber? Only to find that, when fully awake, all knots had been retied, winding a thick blanket of confusing logic around my clear head. In my present state, the tantalising clarity/ confusion/ clarity/ confusion/ clarity/ confusion/ clarity/ confusion/ ran on and on, in and out, and kept my head on the pillow for a long time.

I sensed that a contradiction was fuelling this motor and dragging me out of my dreams: Something H.D. had said the night before, something to do with a *Real-o-meter*, and the need to delve down through "the mud and slush of opinion, and prejudice, and tradition, and delusion, and appearance, till we come to a hard bottom and

37

rocks in place, which we can call reality, and say, This is, and no mistake, a place where you might found a wall or a state."

Seeing the need for a Real-o-meter, I tried to picture it: a blinding, white hot armour plated shredding probe, with its end-point located at infinity. Sharp enough to bore through the age-old lines of written and rhetorical sediment, the Real-o-meter would shred to futility any attempt to write it's instruction manual, taking with it the inherent contradiction between H.D's neologism and it's printed appearance. The friction between this, my construction, and the function of the Real-o-meter could lull me into that sleepy antagonistic bliss forever, if I'd allow it. I finally conceded, and it was not my dreamlike clarity, but my waking confusion that drove me on, up and out of bed.

Even now, my hunger, as ever, was pushed aside by my urges: the urge to lay chewing on the words and thoughts going through my head had been replaced by the urge to swim (and prompted by the increasing heat inside the house). I opened a drawer and took out a small black bag, that contained a clean white towel and my black swimming shorts, and following this latest obsession like a sleepwalker, I walked back out of the house, through the blue gate and into the neighbouring park. Crossing from one side to the other, I felt a sense of time coming back to me, and, noticing that I was the only person around, walked towards the open-air pool with the fear that it was so early in the morning that it would surely be closed for the public. A blackbird, in the finishing its dawn call, attracted my attention towards the tree-tops, all of which seemed to have become fantastically full and green that morning. The grass was like a well kept, lush lawn, and I could sense that the whole park, though dead to the world, was more abundant and full of life than I'd ever noticed before.

The pool's doors weren't open. Contrary to my fears of closure, there *were* no doors. In fact, all the walls around the pool had been taken down in the few weeks I had been away. I wondered how and why they had managed to find the means to achieve this in such a short time, but was simply glad that they had. Things that are right have no need for justification.

I had always felt quite unwelcome at the pool, having to pass through a high gate in the high fence surrounding it, then go through two sets of glass doors, and then pass through a stainless steel tourniquet with its LED number increasing by one as I did, after having paid the required entrance fee. All these obstacles had been removed, and the thick cool lawn of the park ran all the way up to the tiled edge of the pool and under the stilts of the changing cabins. I was surprised at how the place had been completely rethought *and* remade in such a short space of time.

What's more: the pool was completely empty. I was used to even the early morning hours being occupied by the most motivated lap-crawlers, but today the need to fit in so many laps in so much time before going to work to fulfill so many tasks, the contagious pressure of performance that I had become quite adverse to, was not present in this air.

THE MIDDLE OF NOWHERE

There was no one else was in the pool: no pressure of the speed of others, forcing me to 'keep up'. I was the only visitor, save for one man at the other end who reclined in a deck-chair on the grass, and judging on his neat, uniform clothes, seemed to hold some kind of position there. I waved to him, assuming that any kind of acknowledgement of my presence would be enough to allow me to go ahead and swim. The permissive nature of the pool's layout confused me a little, surely such a privileged situation came with a catch. Yet the man did not wave back, or make any kind of signal to show that he had seen me. It seemed so early and quiet that the pool MUST be closed; nevertheless, I tried to get on as usual, though extremely self-consciously, until the man would notice me and ask me to leave.

Coming out of the cabin, I walked back to the deep end of the pool, chose a lane, and let myself down into the water to hang on to the side and stretch my jetlagged muscles in the water before starting to swim. I kept an eye on the man in the deckchair the whole time, for any sign of reaction, but only when I gently lowered myself to break the surface of the warm water, did he look up suddenly and stare in my direction, his eyebrows slightly frowned and his eyes squinting to get a better look. His expression was that of slight surprise mixed with a large portion of incomprehension, as though he had expected a large animal to have fallen into the pool, and along with this, could not understand how the form of this animal actually resembled another man, like himself.

He stood up, and seemed rather astonished, until he acknowledged himself and tried to watch less obviously. Simply assuming that I had startled him from his sleep, I began to swim my leisurely breast-stroke, enjoying the perfect temperature of the water, the endless view of green around me, and the sounds of the mass of birds engaged in the ritual dawn chorus. Perhaps it was the focus of the early morning, but I had never heard that many birds so clearly, all at once. It seemed like, with the right knowledge, I could distinguish each bird from the next, and hear exactly from which direction each call was coming.

I dived, and swam half a lap underwater, enjoying the muffled enclosed sound. Ever since I was young, and had listened to the tons of beach shingle underwater being swept back and forward by the sea, I would make a habit out of lying on my back for long periods, listening to the sounds of that part of the world that was unknown to me, knowledge of which came only through my ears, and even so completely distorted by being carried on water. It was the natural filtering of certain frequencies, the distortion that fascinated me, along with the focus of sensory deprivation. I came up for air, and closed my eyes and swam length after slow length on my back, with light being filtered deep dark red through my eyelids, and my ears under water, listening to myself breathing deeply, gently bumping my head when I reached one end of the pool, turning around and continuing back, as undisturbed as possible. After a while I opened my eyes again and looked up at the clear blue sky and the edges of the trees in the corners of my eyes. I softly bumped my head once more, and stopped, taking time to regain the sense of my surroundings, looking back across the pool to see the guard still staring at me, as though I was guilty of swimming all those lengths at such a slow pace. I decided to swim over and ask whether anything was wrong.

Halfway through the length, I exaggerated the friendliness in my voice, and called out "Good morning!"

The man seemed even more startled at hearing his own language, or any language, for that matter, to come from that direction. He looked confused, but bravely stuttered a response: "G-good morning."

"You look like I'm doing something wrong. Is everything OK?" I asked as I swam up to him.

"I don't know you, do I?" the man replied. This seemed like a strange question: there must be a few hundred people coming to the pool every day, especially in this weather.

"Should you?" I asked, thinking that perhaps the new-look pool came with a strict new-look membership. Then again, if it was that recent, *and* if they had taken down all the walls, this must have been a common misunderstanding and the man would not have been staring in surprise for so long.

"What do you mean 'Should I?' How can I not know you?"

"Well, I don't come here that often, and I've never seen you here before either, to be honest," I replied, trying to leave the smart-alec out of my voice.

"I'm sorry, I didn't mean to be rude. We just don't get your types aroun... I've never met someone like you bef... Oh, I'm really sorry, I didn't mean to stare. Excuse me for being such a bad host. You must have come such a long way!"

"Not really. I live on the other side of the park."

Once again he began to stare in disbelief and the frown of incomprehension returned to his forehead. Slowly, the suspicion arose in me that this man was some kind of eccentric. His strange reactions to me were belied by his appearance. The thing was, he was dressed in a black suit, that, from a distance

45

of 50 metres, I had mistaken for a uniform. I reached the edge of the pool, and leant on my forearms at its edge. From that close, it was clear that his suit was cut with such a great deal of attention and in such a way that it was far from being a one-size-fits-many, off-the-peg uniform. His suit simply hung in a way on his body that it clearly could not have been made for anyone but himself. A complementary white shirt with winged collar, and a simple thin white silk tie, in a slightly different shade of white, was just enough to see that it was an intentional difference, and not born of any kind of necessity. Even in this heat, he actually looked very comfortable in the thin fabric of the suit, and the tie was knotted in such a way that it was clear that he dressed with that much care, every day. It was not his *idea* of how a tie should be tied, it was simply *tied*, as much as his hair was *combed*, his nails *kept* and his shoes *clean*. Regardless of the frown of the moment, his face had a clear expression, with a peculiarly pleasant and friendly look about his eyes—an expression which was quite new to me then, though I soon became familiar with it. For the rest, he was dark-haired and tanned, and obviously used to exercising his muscles, with nothing rough or coarse about him. In short, he seemed to be some specially manly and refined young gentleman, playing pool-guard for his own eccentric entertainment.

I felt like I must make some conversation; so I pointed through the trees, to the West End of the park, and said: "They certainly managed to finish that school quickly. When I was here last, it was still covered in scaffolding and under construction, a 'CDC' (Child Development Centre) in the making. It doesn't seem to be the product of successive interventions of government rulings after all, or built according to the 'taste' of architecture that I had been afraid of. It's fantastic that it's been given that much space to breathe. They've taken down all the buildings around it, too. You can see right through it from here, it looks as though the park continues behind it."

The longer I looked, the more I saw.

Children Along the Way

Observing one change led to seeing another, and another, until I became obsessed with the increasing altered details of the surroundings that I took for granted, for so long.

He looked down the length of my dripping arm, past my pointing finger, in order to be sure of which building I was talking about. It was a long building, of four high storeys, with a very fine skeletal, and obviously modular construction, that became absorbed by the whole instead of dictating it's appearance. The building was covered with hand-pulled sheets of slightly tinted glass, which shimmered in their inconsistencies.

"The park does go on, and yes, it is the only building of its size in this area. The Restoration transformed the building back to its original state. At the same time the present state is also rather unique, in that it has been worn by use, and become slowly more beautiful and absorbed by its surroundings and function."

I found myself saying, almost against my will, "How old is it?"

"Oh not very old," he said: "it was built, at least restored, in 2116."

N

as in NEUROLOGY: So, he knows it's better to have a competent perception, but he still maintains that everything that counts in the world in the realm of the mind is open to a double reading, provided that it is not something done randomly as a someone self-taught might. Rather, it's something that one undertakes starting from one's problems taken from elsewhere. Deleuze means that it's on the basis of being a philosopher that he has a non-musical perception of music, which makes music extraordinarily stirring for him. Similarly, it's on the basis of being a musician, a painter, this or that, that one can undertake a non-philosophical reading of philosophy. If this second reading (which is not second) did not occur, if there weren't these two, simultaneous readings, it's like both wings on a bird, the need for two readings together. Moreover, Deleuze argues that even a philosopher must learn to read a great philosopher non-philosophically. The typical example for him is yet again Spinoza: reading Spinoza in paperback, whenever and wherever one can, for Deleuze, creates as much emotion as a great musical work. And to some extent, he says, the question is not understanding since in the courses that Deleuze used to give, it was so clear that sometimes the students understood, sometimes they did not; and we are all like that, sometimes understanding, sometimes not. Deleuze comes back to Parnet's question on science that he sees the same way: to some extent, one is always at the extreme [pointe] of one's ignorance, which is exactly where one must settle in [s'installer], at the extreme of one's knowledge or one's ignorance, which is the same thing, in order to have something to say. If he waited to know what he was going to write, Deleuze says, literally, if he waited to know what he was talking about, then he would always have to wait because what he would say would have no interest. But if he speaks from this very border between knowing and non-knowing, it's there that one must settle in to have something to say.

O

as in OPERA: Parnet points out that Châtelet worked while listening to opera, to which Deleuze says, first, he couldn't do that, and he's not so sure that Châtelet did while working, maybe, and of course, when he entertained people at his home. Opera sometimes covered over what people were saying when he'd had enough, but for Deleuze, that's not how it works for him. But, he says that he would prefer to turn the question more in his own favor by transforming it into: what is it that creates a community between a popular song and a musical work of art? That's a subject that Deleuze finds fascinating. The case of Edith Piaf, for example: Deleuze considers her to be a great 'chanteuse', with an extraordinary voice; moreover, she has this way of singing off-key and then constantly catching the false note and making it right, this kind of system in imbalance that constantly is catching and making itself right. For Deleuze, this seems to be the case in any style. This is something Deleuze likes a lot because it's the question he poses about everything on the level of the popular song: he wonders, what does it bring to me that is innovative [de nouveau]? Especially in the productions, they bring something innovative. If it's been done 10, 100, 1000 times, maybe even done quite well, Deleuze understands then what Robbe-Grillet said: Balzac was obviously a great writer, but what interest is there in creating novels today like Balzac created them? Moreover, that practice sullies Balzac's novels, and that's how it is in everything. What Deleuze found particularly moving in Piaf was that she introduced something innovative in relation to the preceding generation, Frehel and Adabia, even in her self-presentation, and in her voice. That's not to be interpreted in the sense of fashion, but just the opposite: what's innovative is something that's not fashionable, perhaps it will become so, but it's not fashionable since people don't expect it.

1

The Aesthetics of Distribution (2)

A REAR GUARD

An interview with Mark Wigley
by David Reinfurt

Recorded at Columbia University,
April 2007.

DAVID REINFURT: I first found your writing through 'Network Fever'[2] and 'Recycling Recycling',[3] two texts which recount partially forgotten, or willfully ignored, architectural discourses around networks and ecology, respectively. In 'Recycling Recycling', you describe:

> Recycling allows the same materials to be transformed from one object to another, such that the materials move, as he puts it, through cultural space. Materials are, as it were, morphed through space and time. Culture is understood as a set of flows. The culture of architecture is but a rhythmic ecology of images, even if they are not simply understood as visual images. Architecture becomes plastic, a morphing communication system that moves around the globe and in so doing defines a space, an artificial nature that is inhabited on an everyday basis.

And continue:

> Ecology is a question of images in the end, images of architecture and the architecture of images … Lectures like this one, for example, are no more than the exchange of certain kinds of images. We need to think about the politics of such exchanges. More precisely, we have to think about the intersection between such institutionalised technologies of imagery and institutions (like this School of Architecture here in Auckland) which are themselves technologies with specific agendas and mechanisms to realise those agendas.

Now that you are Dean of the Columbia University Graduate School of Architecture, Planning and Preservation (GSAPP), how do you reconcile your previous critical position in relation to institutions with your current job description?

MARK WIGLEY: I ran away from a tenured position at Princeton University School of Architecture seven or eight years ago. Then after about four years at Columbia, I find myself as Dean. So this question is on everybody's mind, including my own.

Running a school is a bit like cooking or gardening—what matters is not so much the specific food or the specific plants, but the kind of evolution, the various speeds of evolution and the uncontrolled reactions between elements. What you are looking for in a school of architecture is productive mutations. Each and every micro-decision is then a theoretical act and the most miniscule rearrangement of the budget can be understood precisely in ecological terms.

Then, an architect is somebody who is reluctantly invited into a situation because the people who should be in control of the situation are not. The parents who should be controlling the house no longer know what to do with the bedroom that's been vacated by the daughter who has gone to college. The city that should be in control, financially, politically, and so on, doesn't know what kind of library would satisfy all of the complex constituents. The architect is called into an overwhelming situation, with a unique form of intelligence, to combine things that do not belong together.

The architect is in a state of calm exactly when everybody else is overwhelmed, which is why architects live at a different rhythm, they don't eat at the same time as other people, they don't work at the same time, they don't talk to other people and they don't retire. What they are doing is illegal, impossible, against the rules, unruly. And that unique form of thinking provides a plausible organizational structure which will allow conflicting forces to operate. This is why I think the intelligence of the architect is precious and unique and also, why it is absolutely not paid and treated with great suspicion.

If an architecture school is for producing that kind of intelligence, then how, in a university, the very home of rational thought, do you create a space for a promiscuous optimism? Well, if you deeply celebrate this form of intelligence, almost monumentalize it, you will create both the conditions required for this kind of thought to occur and also the conditions required for such a way of thinking to evolve. So that's why for me, being essentially a historian of the way architects think, to help guide a school is to directly operate in the realm of thought.

DR: From the inside of the school, it seems that you foster an environment that is necessarily out of your control and where the boundary is blurred between the structure and what grows out of it —I think maybe that's the point. So then, practically, how do you create this kind of situation?

MW: This requires another illicit combination —an intense micro-management and an intense relaxation. You micro-manage certain key variables in the belief that it will allow the unexpected to flourish. And when it happens, you don't interfere. So, you micro-manage in order to reach a space you can't control and also, you control absolutely, like a dictator, in order to be surprised. So you could say, 'You're a control freak.' But, there are two kinds of control freaks: a control freak who wants to limit the numbers of surprises in life and a control freak who wants to maximize them. For a while, they might not look so different, but in the end there's a big difference . . .

Laughter

. . . because one is happy when the surprises arrive and the other gets angry.

DR: In preparing for this interview, I read your recent essay 'The Space of Exposure' from the catalog for Wolfgang Tillmans' show in the Hammer Museum at UCLA.[4] In it, you describe a particular quality of these photographs:

> In each case, all evidence of rearrangement is removed so that the staged scenes are experienced as found, and the found scenes are experienced as precisely arranged.
>
> These photographs relentlessly blur found and constructed—carefully remaining ambiguously between the capturing of an available instant, as in Henri Cartier Bresson's work, and the slow labor of total constructions, as in Jeff Wall's work, to cite a couple of too obvious paradigms of the extremes. If photographers like Cartier-Bresson steal the image and those like Wall painstakingly build it, Tillmans drifts ambiguously between the taking and making, and places the viewer in the same mode. No clue is offered as to the choreographing of each scene, preserving the sense of a rich found world. So each image appears halfway between the world and the photographer, an image not simply received from the world onto the sensitive film in the camera, but an image just as much coming out from the sensitive photographer—an image, in the end, of the photographer in the world. As much projected out through the film onto the world as received onto the film from the world. The construction begins to with the seemingly transparent but actually distorting glass of the lens itself. When pressed on this point, Tillmans remarks that 'photography always lies about what is in front of the camera but never lies about what is behind.'

I'm struck by how this idea resonates with what you describe in 'Recycling Recycling'—where the transformation of one kind of image into another and its relentless circulation work to collapse categories of found, made and recycled. So I wonder, does that thinking influence the way that you run the School?

MW: Well, Wolfgang Tillmans is a very interesting photographer—both in the doubt that he constructs between what's found and what's made and also in this profound observation that the image is always ruthlessly honest to what's going on for the photographer and ruthlessly dishonest with regard to the world. Photographic realism then becomes a psychological category; it is no longer the world of accepted facts, instead realism actually becomes the desire.

So here you have a photographer who appears to be hardly taking the photograph; he seems to be simply picking up the facts. In that sense, his work can be associated with the long tradition of photographic realism, but already we have to hesitate. His work puts the symptoms of realism —technical considerations like framing, timing, duration of the exposure, etcetera that normally conspire to give the photograph the kind of quasi-truth of function—into question by this simple thought: The camera always lies about what's in front of it and always tells the truth about what's behind it.

In architecture, we have an interesting parallel—architecture has always had a cultural responsibility to the category of realism. One of its jobs has been to make a picture, an image in the world that was of the truth of the world, but so much so that it was not in the world like anything else.

The obvious example is a classical temple. A classical temple is supposed to be beautiful, because its proportions resonate with the cosmic harmony of the Universe. But it also has the irony of saying it's an object in the world that so perfectly represents the world that it actually escapes the world. The temple is literally put onto a little platform so it can jump off into space. It's purely about the image.

DR: Which recalls the story that you tell in 'Recycling Recycling' describing a lecture given by artist, Independent Group member and 'Father of Pop'[5] John McHale at the ICA in London in 1961 called 'The Plastic Parthenon'. In this talk, McHale describes how plastic replicas of architectural monuments end up with more cultural weight than the buildings they depict:

> In this new environment, a new economy, if not ecology, operates. Products become as expendable as images. Indeed, products are images. Even buildings succumb to the logic of obsolescence rather than scarcity. The 'machine aesthetic' of the so called International Style is described as just that, an aesthetic, an 'image of functional modernity rather than its actuality,' an image that could circulate the globe in an unprecedented way but will give way to other images.

MW: Well, architecture has always offered a stabilizing image in an overwhelming world. The world is perceived to be an abundant confusion of forces and architecture is an image of calm in the face of these—it has a longer time frame, it stays the same, it's solid.

Now, in a highly experimental school of architecture like Columbia, you are obviously challenging that function and are therefore trying to stay closer to the wilderness, closer to the world. You take a group of architects and say: 'What makes you an architect is that you can look into the face of a storm, an overwhelming promiscuity of ideas, forces, images, and so on; and you have a special gift to remain calm and to calmly draw an illegal, irresponsible, indefensible, unrationalizable figure around which all these different forces can be seen to harmoniously gather or linger for a while. But we are going to ask you to delay that calming gesture as much as possible.'

Your question then makes me wonder about the relationship between the kind of hesitation that Tillmans' photographs introduce and the hesitation that's produced by, and required of, our students. Hesitation is required by asking our students to delay before fixing the uncertainty, to live longer in the wild. And hesitation is produced by the best of them when their work interrupts our routines and for a moment invites us to move sideways. The best architecture makes these overwhelming forces seem, at least for a moment, just a little bit, attractive.

A piece of architecture is an articulate building, a building that talks—a building that says things about itself and about the world. And that means that architecture is that discipline that believes objects talk, and talk about the world; a discipline devoted to the possibility of a synergy between the material and the immaterial, between thoughts, ideas and objects.

It's really easy to reverse it, to see objects —the built environment—as just a kind of a trace, a visible remainder of intelligence. But not intelligence as in 'an intelligent thought', but rather, intelligence itself.

DR: I've heard intelligence described as the ability to hold two divergent thoughts completely in your mind at one time, without sacrificing the complexity of either.

MW: In architecture, it's more like 20 divergent thoughts. But when people say the ability of intelligence is to hold two opposite thoughts in your head at the same time, they might find what an architect does quite shocking. The whole principle of architectural education is to suspend the students in a protected space in which this kind of lack of definition to thinking is provoked, supported and incubated.

DR: This is one of the things I find compelling about architecture and architects—this fanatically comprehensive way of thinking, which assimilates everything, all the time. And still retains the desire and hubris to actually want to do everything. It's absurd, fantastic and optimistic.

MW: And that seems like a paradox at the beginning, right? The one group in our community dedicated to objects that never change, don't move and even represent stability (the buildings)—cultivate absolute instability.

Not instability in the sense of shakiness, blurriness or vulnerability, but instability in the sense of freedom and openness to difference, to otherness. That's really the most radical form of instability—to be comfortable with 'the other'. That's what it is to live in a city, of course, to embrace 'the other'.

Of course, to make an encounter with 'the other', there's also a sort of preservation of the self. You can't call the other 'the other', without, at the same time, reinforcing your self. The great gesture by which you embrace 'the other' is also the gesture by which you harden your own definition.

So, architectural intelligence, if you like, or the way that architects are asked to think—it's not just that they think that way, but that they are required to think that way—they hesitate on that line between embracing the outside, 'the other', and sealing in and constructing the inside. That's what architecture is—it's about walls; it's about lines; it's inside and outside. You cannot imagine a greater responsibility. And yet, in our cultural life, the architect is a figure of absolute unimportance, professionally and so on. It's a responsibility that's almost medieval. There has to be a group in our culture who protect the definition of inside/outside and who hover on the threshold and define the line. And that's what architects do, like monks.

It's a bad analogy, because monks don't have a good time; but, like monks, we only ever hang around with other architects. We don't get outside. We don't have weekends. There's no money involved. There's always higher ambition. We wear black. We don't smile. And so on and so on. There's a privacy to being a monk. Everybody admires a monk, but wouldn't want to be one. So, monks we are.

DR: Returning to the circulation of architectural images, you open the essay 'Network Fever' with:

> We are constantly surrounded by talk of networks. Every third message, article, and advertisement seems to be about one network or another. We are surrounded, that is, by talk on networks about networks. It is as if our technologies feed on a kind of narcissistic self-reflection. Everyone has become a kind of expert, ready to discuss the different types of nets (computer, television, telephone, airline, radio, beeper, bank ...) or scales (global, national, infra, local, home ...) or modes (cable, wireless, digital, optical ...). And where would we be without our opinions about the Internet, a net of nets against which all others are now referenced?

And in 'Recycling Recycling', you assert:

> It becomes ever more obvious that architecture is almost literally carved into the flow of images.

Given this background, then how does publishing work at the School? Specifically, can you describe the Columbia Laboratory for Architectural Broadcasting (C-Lab) and its bi-monthly journal,

Volume? What are the strategies, modes and vehicles for circulating the images that the School produces?

MW: If the architect is a public intellectual, then that thinking only has currency if it's launched to the outside. So, publications for a school of architecture are the 'making public', bringing the inside of the school to the outside. They are not an optional extra.

A school throws images into the world and C-Lab is a machine for throwing things. Whatever it throws has to be a different kind of throw and a different kind of object and a different kind of image. For example, *Volume* is the product of a triangular collaboration between a school with C-Lab inside it, an architect's office (Rem Koolhaas) with a research unit inside it, and ARCHIS, an architectural foundation with a magazine inside it.

C-Lab is one of a series of research laboratories which sit on the boundary between the inside and the outside of the School. I'm deeply committed to this concept of a perforated school, where every line between inside and outside, between architectural training and professional practice, between quiet isolation and noisy confusion are challenged and rethought.

In order to do this, you need what seems to be its opposite—a detailed knowledge of the traditions that have generated a sense of certainty in the discipline. So, we have the best architecture library in the world at the base of Avery Hall (home of the GSAPP at Columbia University.) *Volume*, if it is any good, will find its way back into the library.

DR: Part of the Architectural Broadcasting program at C-Lab includes a series of irregular 15-second video clips released on its website (c-lab.columbia.edu). Can you describe how this kind of publishing intersects with something like *Volume*, and if there are any other specific networks of circulation—weblogs, mailing lists, events—planned for the future?

MW: Maybe it's just a conservative statement, but I think most of the blog culture is in a very early stage and one can't be sure that it's leading anywhere in particular. Most of the blog space seems devoted to absorbing free radical energy. It has a great capacity to neutralize any line of thought, when, in theory, blog space could consolidate new trajectories of thought, reinforce and empower those trajectories in an explosive way. But the dominant effect is to absorb energy. At this moment, blog space is a deeply conservative territory.

DR: Maybe that brings us back to the ecological argument from 'Recycling Recycling' ...

> While taking account of this new architecture, it would be a mistake to recycle recycling today without understanding the extent to which the overt politics of ecology, which is to say the equitable management of resources, preserves particular regressive ideological formations.

MW: It's exactly to do with that. The way that things circulate in blog space produces a kind of entropy of ambition. In Robert Smithson's famous definition of entropy, you take some black sand and some white sand, you shake it up and once you've shaken it up, you cannot return.

I think that almost anything launched into blog space with a certain energy, loses that energy very quickly. It is, therefore, a very efficient political machine. While MoveOn.org looked like a new form of political organization, it's not just that the election was won by the other side, but in some sort of Machiavellian sense, that MoveOn energy actually defused itself. In fact, this was largely represented by the candidate receiving most of that energy, Howard Dean, who himself famously exploded one day.[6]

Whereas the 15-second video which C-Lab is releasing might be not so easily consumed. In a YouTube environment, this becomes almost heroically short. With through-put and bandwidth, surely the average video length is increasing steadily; as it does, YouTube's capacity to make any image unimportant grows. In other words, an image can appear to grow in intensity—a Zinedine Zidane video can dominate for a while, but its death is always built in. The only question is, what's the nature of the death of this image.

This experiment with short-term video creates, then—kind of back where nobody's looking—a territory that might be seen as technologically primitive. It becomes, with every passing minute, more and more interesting. Part of what C-Lab can do is to occupy these seemingly vestigial domains.

For the moment, I think we're going to be hanging back there, in the same way that schools of architecture are becoming interested in black and white photography, or hand drawings. There's a kind of a rear guard experimentalism going on.

NOTES
1. Looking out from the rear of their rocket five hours and six minutes into the journey, the crew of NASA's Apollo 17 found themselves perfectly aligned between the sun and the earth, yielding a view of the full disc of the earth completely illuminated by the sun. This 70 mm photograph was the first clear image of the entire earth, floating alone in a deep and black space—a small, lonely and finite whole system of weather, land, water and people. This image catalalyzed the emergent ecology movement and soon found itself reproduced and recycled endlessly from flags to tshirts to posters to magazines. According to NASA archivist Mike Gentry, this image may be the most widely circulated photographic image ever.
2. Published in *Grey Room*, Summer 2001, No. 04, pp. 82–122.
3. The full text of this essay is also online here: http://www.architecture.auckland.ac.nz/common/library/1995/11/i4/THEHTML/keynotes/wigley/front.htm.
4. From 'The Space of Exposure' in *Wolfang Tillmans*, an exhibition catalogue produced with The Hammer Museum, Los Angeles and the Museum of Contemporary Art, Chicago, 2006.
5. British architectural critic Reyner Banham famously referred to John McHale as the 'scholar-artist, this "Father of Pop"' as described in *The Expendable Ikon: Works by John McHale*, an Albright Knox catalogue, 1984.
6. Howard Dean's campaign for president suffered a blow when a last-minute surge by rivals John Kerry and John Edwards led to an embarrassing third-place defeat in the 2004 Iowa Democratic caucuses. Due to a mix of technical difficulties and frustration while delivering his concession speech, Dean burst into what became known as 'The Scream' —a prolonged post-verbal utterance, which was circulated relentlessly in countless media, with disastourous effects for Dean's campaign. The video footage can currently be found on YouTube.

as in PROFESSOR: Deleuze says that even on the level of ambition, of being the leader of a 'school' [Here he sighs]—it's awful, it creates so many worries. One has to become Machiavellian to lead it all, and then for Deleuze himself, he despises that. For him, the 'school' is the opposite of a movement. He gives a simple example: Surrealism was a 'school', with scores settled, trials, exclusions, etc., Breton as the leader; whereas Dada was a movement. Deleuze says that if he had an ideal, it would be to participate in a movement. For Deleuze, relations with students means to teach them that they must be happy with their solitude. That, says Deleuze, was his role as a professor.

DECORATION *

████████████████████████████ decoration and the role that decoration plays within the design.

████████████████ designers are very categorical, very anarchical, very radical.

████████████████ "Decoration as we imagine it involves disregard of the support structure as the basic structure of the design. People have always 'believed' in the basic structure; they have always believed that that structure 'had' to exist; they have always believed in the design as a succession of moments and in the unalienability of mental structures, as earnestly as they have believed in the principle of causality. We tend to imagine the design as a series of accidents that come together by chance; we imagine a possible sum, not an inevitable story. And what we believe holds this story of accidents together and gives it meaning, is that every accident has a formal, decorative identity. A ████████ table is decoration. Structure and decoration are one thing."

████████████████████████████ decoration as a key element in the reinvention of figuration and of image. ████████ "In a traditionally designed object the surface is a single unit. Until four of five years ago people devoted all their energy to making surfaces homogeneous, associable, and continuous. Today the tendency is to see the design not so much as a unit but as a sum of parts. We have almost come to study the cells that make up objects more than the objects themselves. Materials and decoration are cells of objects, and they are part of this process."

This change of attitude corresponds to a dive from the certainties of the macrocosm to the virtual universe of particles, from a world borne by the laws of deterministic logic to a world interpreted through the hypotheses of probability. Objects are no longer designed from the outside according to a certain idea of structure; they are genetically engineered from the inside in an inverse process that adapts the final structure to the variable logic of its constituent parts.

At this point the question at issue is no longer mere formal innovation – adding, subtracting, or changing the direction of things – but the radical subversion of the epistemology of the design. The design is no longer a solution, but a hypothesis. It is not a definitive declaration, but a stage, a transitory moment, a container of possibilities, an unstable living form that evolves in time.

████████████████████ decoration is fundamental, and that it coincides with the search for a future aesthetic. ████████ "Functionalism has now become a

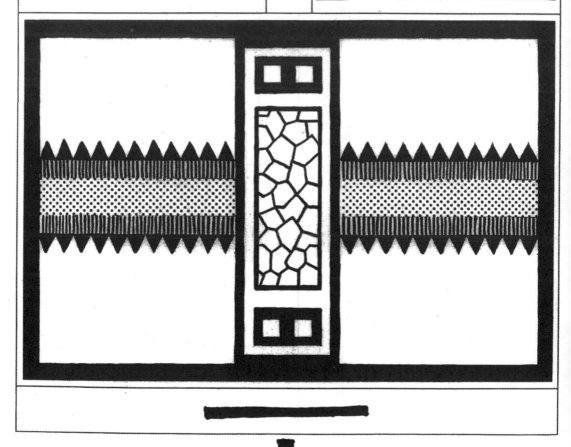

style, just as Japanese technological design is a style. But no one ever said that things have to be that way. With electronics, we are rapidly moving toward another kind of technology that involves other possibilities, other facilities, and a different relationship to the world – more sophisticated, more elastic, less moralizing, and less austere. Electronics is also decoration, play, color. Decoration belongs to the world of electronics just as functionalism belonged to that of the machine."

████████furniture – ████████████████████ – is built by decoration. The works of ████████ designers are assemblages, agglomerates, multitudes, clusters, heaps, deposits of decorations that overlap, intersect, add up and flow together, but always maintain their linguistic independence. They are never subordinated to one another and they are never subordinated to the design.

Typical ████████ decoration is generally nondirectional, homogeneous, repeatable, abstract. It tends to disrupt the stability of static structures and, suggesting a hypothetical expansion of the pattern in all directions, it blurs the object's outlines. It is born with the design as an organic image of its molecular structure. It comes to the surface with the same logical naturalness as the grain in a piece of wood. The truly disconcerting thing is its obvious, peremptory "necessity."

Looking at ████████ patterns one gets the impression that they have always existed as part of the natural order of things – however weird – just like undulated sheet metal, TV, advertising, airplanes and football. They are so obvious that virtually no one has even talked about them in the two-hundred-odd publications that have come out in a year and half since their public début.

The special qualities of ████████ decorations are their inert, aphonic neutrality, their deliberate lack of learned references (which make it possible to keep a clear mind and to glide over them weightless), and their brutal figurative indifference. These quasi-mechanical, assembly-line-like qualities are the outcome of the avalanche of brain-racking inquiry, checks, double-checks, trials and research ██████

████ I remember all too well seeing friends' offices overwhelmed by thousands of xeroxes of almost identical patterns, and listening to endless discussions – broken by long, very Japanese silences – over what to print and whether in positive or negative. Most of the patterns are photographic enlargements of the most disparate "sets" of things, such as coffee beans, rice, pasta, salad, clay, liquid surfaces or Letraset figures. Some are line drawings of photographs or of other drawings; others are ink or dot-pattern drawings. Some were born as "independent," generic patterns; others are motivated and "specific," like ████████ wicked, hard, aggressive patterns bristling with edges and points, to contrast with soft, undulating forms and pastel shades in the designs ██████████████████

███ a kind of natural decorative genius – anarchic, highly sensitive, wild, abstruse, capable of turning out extraordinary drawings at the frantic pace of a computer. ████ visual research is unrestrained, it absorbs everything like a sponge and nothing in particular. In the end it's the collage that counts.

████ hard, aggressive, acid patterns, ████ harsh, sharp, flat colors, ████ broad, black, angular mark make no compromise. They are impervious to logic, and they are so tight that they verge on agoraphobia. They embrace Africa, Cubism, Futurism, and Art Déco; India, graffiti, jungles and town; science fiction, caricature, aborigenes, and Japanese comics. They are enthusiastic, explosive, exalted, elated, as striking as neon in a tropical night. Thinking about them gives you the creeps. ████████████ decoration lays bare the soul of things.

* This is a version of Ettore Sottsass's statement on decoration which originally appeared in *Memphis: Research, Experiences, Results, Failures and Successes of New Design* (1984), altered in 2006 by Justin Beal.

As an industrial design student I was always irritated by the Memphis group. They were the awkward ugly chapter in the history of industrial design at the onset of postmodernism; the moment when, to someone whose education followed a specific modernist history, everything was overcome with bad taste and poor judgment. It was a problem: something which clearly developed out of a history of modernist and functionalist design suddenly turned that history on its head. In Memphis's work, the ethics of functionalism are completely denied—materials are used 'dishonestly', structure is concealed, and function follows form. Humour and poor taste win out over the gravitas commonly associated with modern design. Now, however, looking at that work from another vantage point—as a sculptor with a certain investment in a history of design—Memphis suddenly seems more like an answer than a problem; an answer to a question which asks how furniture and sculpture might merge.

The pieces I am particularly interested in actually preceded Memphis by nearly 25 years: Ettore Sottsass's plastic laminate furniture prototypes from the late 1960s (above). These prototypes evolved into the Superbox wardrobes produced by Poltronova in 1968—big mono- lithic cabinets that appear functionless at first, like oversized, garishly-decorated plinths, or minimalist sculpture gone awry. In fact they are cabinets with concealed hinges. Sottsass photographed the cabinets with a variety of props—foam watermelons, hi-fi stereo equipment, and a naked young woman. The photographs give no indication of what function the Superbox might serve, nor how they might be deployed in a domestic environment.

The bright striped plastic laminates of these cabinets prefigured a series of plastic laminate stock patterns designed by Sottsass and the rest of the Memphis group—Michele de Lucchi, Christoph Radl, and Nathalie du Pasquier —between 1981 and 1983, with names such as *Serpente*, *Micidial*, *Terrific*, and *Traumatic* (below, clockwise from top left). These laminates were applied to a wide range of furniture and objects which became the signature of what Sottsass dubbed Memphis's 'New International Style'.

Their version of 'New International Style' undermines any straightforward interpretation based on the existing terms of design criticism: it asks something more of its viewer than furniture 'should'. This is what postmodern architecture supposedly tries to do, but is limited by the fact that a building is always foremost a building; an abstract architecture isn't really possible because buildings are simply too literal. An 'object', on the other hand, can effectively float somewhere between sculpture and furniture— between use-value and art-value. It is difficult to read a Superbox as furniture because its function is not immediately apparent. The balance of form and function which constitutes the aesthetic grammar of modernist design is totally upended; use-value is camouflaged beneath a cacophony of patterns and colours.

This furniture, clearly developed with an awareness of and sympathy for accepted modernist lineage, but in equally clear opposition to straight functionalism, describes a grey area where sculpture and furniture can co-exist, where the dialectic collapses. It is tempting to read Sottsass's celebration of decoration as a rebuttal to Adolf Loos and those who followed in his footsteps. In *Ornament and Crime* (1908) Loos famously claimed 'the evolution of culture is synonymous with the removal of ornamentation from objects of everyday use'.

Bearing in mind Loos's outspoken opinions on ornament, consider his 'House for Josephine Baker '(1928, above) alongside Sottsass's early furniture. This design only ever existed as a single model and partial set of plans—the house was never built and it is unclear whether Loos and Baker ever even met—but the proposal suggests an elaborate program (including an indoor pool, a café and an lavish apartment) concealed behind horizontal bands of black and white marble, surely less a meditation on pure form than a pure celebration of surface.

As much as Sottsass's use of ornament appears to break rank with overarching functionalist conventions, it bears a specific connection to the work of another idiosyncratic Italian modernist, Gio Ponti. The decorated furniture Ponti produced in collaboration with designer Piero Fornasetti in 1950s Milan (such as their Radio Record Player, above) in the is another example of this unconditional embrace of ornament. In an essay on Fornasetti, Sottsass likens the exploding imagery in his patterns to the slow-motion explosions of sets and objects which famously close Michelangelo Antonioni's 1970 counterculture epic *Zabriskie Point* (below).

> He applied his thousand stickers, his discoveries, his choices and his pieces of metaphors with incorruptible determination on everything that exists (and whose logic does not even minimally touch him).

Ponti and Fornasetti's collaboration was a further dialogue between form and surface, material and decoration. The works recounted here are both material *and* decoration: the laminates carry an intrinsic pattern in the same manner as, for example, travertine or mahogany —a pattern *within* the material, not on its surface, and the distinction is paramount.

REFERENCES
—Colomina, Beatrice, *Privacy and Publicity: Mass Media and Architecture* (Cambrige: MIT Press, 1994)
—Loos, Adolf, *Ornament and Crime: Selected Essays* (Riverside, CA: Ariadne Press, 1998)
—Radice, Barbara, *Ettore Sottsass: A Critical Biography* (New York: Rizzoli International Publications, 1993)
—Radice, Barbara, *Memphis: Research, Experiences, Results, Failures and Successes of New Design* (New York: Rizzoli International Publications, 1984)
—Sottsass, Ettore, 'The Fornasetti World' in· Patrick Mauriès (ed.), *Fornasetti: Designer of Dreams* (London: Thames & Hudson, 1991)

as in QUESTION: Parnet states that philosophy for Deleuze serves to pose questions and problems, and that questions are constructed, with their purpose being not to answer them, but to leave these questions behind. So, for example, leaving the history of philosophy behind meant creating new questions. In an interview, one doesn't ask Deleuze questions really.

The motto of the Caretaker shall be

管理员的口号是

take care

请当心

ARTIFICIAL LANGUAGE

by Graham Meyer

In addition to a lot of utopianist rhetoric, Esperanto culture has produced reams of poetry. The Hungarian writer Kálmán Kalocsay was considered the dean of Esperantist poets, and indeed he penned some lines that sound lovely even to the Esperanto-ignorant:

> kaj glitis, glitis, vane ghin mi bridis,
> sur la blanksilka hauhto de l' femur …
>
> [and slid, slid, in vain it bridled me,
> on the white-silk skin of the thigh …][1]

Not Beethoven-worthy verses. But pit their modest artistry versus the idea that Esperanto poetry even exists. Beyond hope, Esperanto has limped along for over a hundred years, in contrast to other attempts at universal languages, like Volapük, whose speakers now numbingly number in the low double digits, or Ido, Esperanto's redheaded stepchild.

Volapük shriveled because its founder was inflexible about changing his creation. He refused, for example, to simplify the phonology by editing out the umlauted vowels, and because Volapük could never mould to the needs of its speakers, it grew mould instead.

Compare universal language attempts with the history of American Sign Language. An ancestor of ASL was the system of 'methodical signs' developed by Abbé Charles Michel de l'Épée to teach to the deaf of Paris, who had bred a pidgin of signs to communicate among themselves. De l'Épée's methodical signs assigned gestures to written French, turning the blooming, buzzing deaf community into masters of taking dictation —effectively stifling their proto-language.

Thomas Hopkins Gallaudet traveled from the United States to Europe in search of methods to teach the deaf, visited de l'Épée's school, and returned home to Connecticut with Laurent Clerc, one of de l'Épée's pupils, riding shotgun. At the school he founded in Hartford, Gallaudet allowed methodical signing to roil around with surviving signs of Old French Sign Language and signs from Martha's Vineyard Sign Language, and the resulting mishmash was the beginning of American Sign Language.

As children began to acquire it as a native language, ASL developed dialects, poetry, and humour. Here's an iconic ASL joke, analogous to 'What's black and white and read all over?'

A deaf man drives up to a train crossing where the gate is down. He waits and waits, but no train goes by. Impatient, the man gets out of his car and walks to the gatekeeper's booth. As he doesn't speak English well, he writes the gatekeeper a note: 'Please but.'

The joke arises from the similarity between the signs for 'but' and 'open the gate', which differ only by the orientation of the palm. (Explaining the joke can't recreate the delight of the two meanings collapsing on each other suddenly, which happens all at once for a native signer.)

The humorous is one bone in the skeleton in the organism of a living language. Vital languages develop and shift through the habits of their native speakers. They're not a simple coding of messages in other media; they're the original medium. This is why de l'Épée's methodical signs failed to gel into a language, and this is why shorthand is dying. If shorthand were anyone's 'native' system of handwriting, it would develop new coinages and usages. Novel abbreviations would arise and 'ds' for 'Dear Sir' would peter out.

Artificial languages aren't incapable of beauty and *jeux des mots*, the French kissing of living tongues. But when novelty comes out of an artificial language, the language steps away from artificiality and into the realm of the human, but mortal.

NOTE
1. Lines 5 and 6 of the 11th of Kalocsay's 'Secret Sonnets'. It gets off-puttingly raunchy after that.

as in RESISTANCE: Parnet asks if we could say that Deleuze, Guattari, and Foucault form networks of concepts like networks of resistance, like a war machine against dominant modes of thought. Deleuze looks visibly embarrassed, and says yes, why not? It would be very nice if it were true. He goes on to reflect on networks: if one doesn't belong to a 'school' there is only the regime of networks, of complicities.

EXTENDED CAPTION

to Alfred Barr's *History*
and Mike Kelley's *Entry Way*

by Howard Singerman

Mike Kelley was an undergraduate art student at the University of Michigan from 1972 to 1976, where he recalls his training as

> quite academic with generous doses of color theory [taught according to 'an Albers-based formal approach'], life and still life drawing and painting, and even exercises in such archaic techniques as egg tempera painting and hand calligraphy. The typical student painting was a gestural abstract formalist composition in the Hans Hofmann manner.[1]

As dry as that sounds, Kelley writes warmly of three of his old Ann Arbor teachers: Gerome Kamrowski, Al Mullen, and Jacqueline Rice. A ceramic sculptor, Jacquie Rice was only briefly at Michigan; she received her MFA in 1970 from the University of Washington (where what seems to have been the first MFA degree was awarded in 1924, to the painter Mabel Lisle Ducasse), and left Ann Arbor for the Rhode Island School of Design just after Kelley graduated. Given the degree, her west coast MFA, and, not coincidentally, her gender, Rice stands for a different kind of history than the one this caption intends to tell, a newer and more contemporary one. The story Kelley's other teachers tell is more modern, and it is one that can be embedded in a history of modern art in Europe. Through them, as Tim Martin has pointed out, Kelley's artistic upbringing can be linked to 'the three European émigrés who most influenced American post-war art education—Josef Albers, Hans Hofmann, and Laszlo Moholy-Nagy.'[2]

Before coming to Ann Arbor in 1946, Gerome Kamrowski had been one of a circle of younger American artists that gathered around the émigré surrealist Roberto Matta in New York in the early 1940s, painting collaborative experimental canvases with Jackson Pollock and William Baziotes. In the twenties, at the University of Minnesota, Kamrowski had been a student of

Cameron Booth, one of Hans Hofmann's earliest American followers, and he went on to study first with Moholy-Nagy in Chicago, at the New Bauhaus, and then with Hofmann himself in New York and Provincetown. Al Mullen taught at Michigan from 1956 until his death in 1983. He had studied with Fernand Leger in Paris on the GI Bill just after World War II, and then with Hofmann in New York, where he had a brief moment of recognition as an 'abstract impressionist' in the early 1950s, and showed on and off into the early 1960s. Kelley's link to the European masters was at least on paper continuous: some form of dotted line, some relatively straight sort of arrow should make up that single degree of separation, but it's not at all clear what that means, or, more to the point, what that meant to him then. Here is a curious piece of evidence—or of something: the 1974 University of Michigan school of art bulletin notes that both Kamrowski and Mullen were students of Hans Hofmann, but Hofmann is spelled wrong in both of the short bios—two fs one n, as though an imposter, or as someone who mattered a long time ago, or whose memory has faded.

It is easy enough to plot Albers, Hofmann, and Moholy-Nagy on the chart on the left; all of them fall somewhere in that tangle of movements and arrows around the horizontal halfway point. Albers and Moholy-Nagy were both at the Bauhaus; they inherited Johannes Itten's famous foundation course from the master in 1923, and moved with the school from Weimar to Dessau in 1926: one could put them just there, toward the right side, circa 1925. Hofmann's site is a little less obvious, less punctual, but in keeping with the sense of development that the diagram makes so palpably clear, it is easy enough to put him in process, to track him along arrows from the Paris of the Fauves—he drew alongside Matisse at the Académie de la Grande Chaumière in 1908 —and then, bearing left, from Paris to the Munich of '(Abstract) Expressionism', of Kandinsky, Jawlensky, and *Der Blaue Reiter*; Hofmann, who was born in Munich, returned from Paris in 1914, and opened his school there the following year. One can almost place Kamrowski, at some moment in the diagram's near future when the arrows from '(Abstract) Expressionism' and '(Abstract) Surrealism' merge. So it should be easy enough to plot Kelley himself, no? But of course, something happens about 1940.

The diagram on the left, the one that I've been working on, is probably familiar to many of you. It is Alfred Barr's diagram of the history of abstract art, published in 1936 in the Museum of Modern Art's exhibition catalogue, *Cubism and Abstract Art*. And even if you haven't seen it, it might still be familiar in the sense that one knows how to read it, in its implications of history and cause. As Edward Tufte has said, both praising and worrying over the Barr diagram, 'Linking lines, arrows, and influence trees bring with them many implicit but powerful assumptions.'[3] It is far less easy to read causality in the image on the right, or even to know what enters into the relationship between one disc, one image, and the next: what frame is its history is offered in, if indeed a history is offered at all? While the assumption of causality, of relationship, is forceful in the Barr diagram, it too might not quite have a history, at least that was Mayer Schapiro's claim very early on. While the catalogue's text and its frontispiece are 'largely an account of historical movements', Schapiro charged in 1937, the story they tell is independent of historical conditions:

> Barr's conception of abstract art remains essentially unhistorical. He gives us, it is true, the dates of every stage in the various movements, as if to enable us to plot a curve, or to follow the emergence of the art year by year, but no connection is drawn between the art and the conditions of the moment.[4]

The red ink, visible in a colour illustration, is supposed to signify something like 'the conditions of the moment', or at least extrinsic causes, but not only is it used sparingly but it turns out *il n'y pas l'hors texte*: industrial modernity arrives only as 'machine aesthetic'—from where or by whom is it aestheticised?; colonialism only as 'negro sculpture'.

That is, what Barr's diagram offers is an autonomous, directed history of art, within which individual artists—names like Hofmann or Moholy-Nagy—are absorbed as positions both in and on that history. Barr's visual lesson (to turn things about) is not unlike Motherwell's verbal, aphoristic one:

> every intelligent painter carries the whole culture of modern painting in his head. It is his real subject, of which anything he paints is both a homage and a critique, and anything he says is a gloss.[5]

Let me let Adorno and Horkheimer, writing in the *Dialectic of Enlightenment*, make their description of the relation of the artist to historical movement a little more complex.

Style represents a promise in every work of art. That which is expressed is subsumed through style into the dominant forms of generality, into the language of music, or painting, or words, in the hope that it will be reconciled thus with the idea of true generality .... It is only in this confrontation with tradition of which style is the record can art express suffering. That factor in a work of art which enables it to transcend reality certainly cannot be detached from style; but it does not consist of the harmony actually realized, of any doubtful unity of form and content, within and without, of individual and society; it is to be found in those features in which discrepancy appears: in the necessary failure of the passionate striving for identity.[6]

Stripped of both artists and history, Barr's graph offers the logic of art, a series of developments, each built out of the last. Whatever the individual artist experiences subjectively of those social forces, must necessarily be routed through style, through a generalisation in the name or shape of tradition, the work is record of the non-coincidence of the specific and the general, of the individual and the social.

What then is the chart on the right? It too is a sort of family tree, and one that might bear some passing, though still family resemblance to Alfred Barr's diagram, the story of becoming an artist. It's a work by Mike Kelley, whose teachers I attempted to plot inside the Barr diagram, entitled *Entry Way (Genealogical Chart)*, a work exhibited alongside his *Educational Complex* at Metro Pictures in 1995. It's difficult to read causality off Kelley's chart, difficult to know how one image, one site, might be related to another, what comes before and after; it's difficult even to know what tense it speaks, or along which axis. *Entry Way* is a rerouted version of those signs at the entrances to towns and cities that announce civic organisations and welcome visitors and newcomers; conventionally, it is not a temporal system, a narrative, but a synchronic one, a collection. In Kelley's revision, however, in its title, its particular gridding, and in those pink and white circles that recall genetic markers, the chart seems to move, haltingly, without an apparent logic, along the diachronic axis, from fathers to sons, from Elks, Lions, and Optimists, through the White Panther Party and John Sinclair's later Rainbow People's Party, whose insignia was a crossed rifle and electric guitar, against a hash pipe, down to Ding-Dong School. Kelley's may be a genealogical chart, one with at least a distant family resemblance to Barr's genealogy of cubism and abstract art, but Kelley's *Entry Way* doesn't get us to or from Hans Hofmann, rather, it charts a very different legacy, another set of influences. Kelley has written that the composition 'was determined by a genealogical chart of my immediate family',[7] but *Entry Way* takes place most clearly, indeed absolutely, outside the immediacy of the family, as that family acts out— or spins out—what the theorist Herbert Marcuse, writing in the 1960s, termed the 'obsolescence of the Freudian concept of man'. For Marcuse, it mattered that Freud's late-nineteenth century subject was formed deep within the family, a crucible whose hierarchical structure left its fundamental dividing mark on the subject, and set in motion the 'multidimensional dynamic by which the individual attained and maintained his own balance between autonomy and heteronomy, freedom and repression, pleasure and pain.'[8] That is, reading Marcuse across the Adorno and Horkheimer I quoted above, style is the man, or at least the family or Freudian man whose suffering and autonomy came from the specifically calibrated, exquisitely divided, lived disjunction of the specific and the general, interior and exterior, individual and social.

For Marcuse in the sixties, whatever interiority might have belonged to the subject in the image of the family seemed to have been fully unfolded, unraveled, in the social. The reality principle now spoke not through the father to the individual child in the family unit, but through 'the daily and nightly media which coordinate one privacy with that of all others, but also through the kids, the peer groups, the colleagues … the playmates, their neighbors, the leader of the gang, the sport, the screen': these are the 'authorities on appropriate mental and physical behavior.'[9] These are new families, meanings, communities, desires. But to see the social fragmented and divided this way, and the subject in a sense undivided—no longer split along the axis of subjectivity but strung along a series of initiations and memberships, situated and interpellated— is to switch subjects, and maybe this is what Kelley's genealogy projects. His subject is not the deep subject of traditional psychoanalysis or for that matter of art history, but the subject of cultural studies. From its title on, *Entry Way* takes place in, indeed it maps rather precisely, what Rosalind Krauss has described as its domain:

> interpellation—or in its more psychological guise, 'identification'—is the very subject-field of a whole new discipline that began to develop in the university … This discipline,

Cultural Studies, has set itself to systematize our understanding of the constitution of human subjects as so many identities that are not so much produced by their accession to a set of social conditions as they are reproduced through a process of (unconscious) identification with preexisting sources of authority and legitimation, whether these sources be people, institutions, or texts.[10]

Kelley's subject in *Entry Way*, and indeed in the various hallways mapped in bowels of his *Educational Complex*, is 'the deposit of a social relationship', a phrase Hal Foster borrows from Michael Baxandall's description of a fifteenth-century painting in order to reattach it to the subject of cultural studies. 'Here, rather than the art, the subject is the "deposit of social relations"': indeed, he is 'flooded by the social.' Foster keeps writing here, and as he continues he works his way toward Kelley's subtitle, and toward just what the juxtaposition of these graphs might show: 'The shift from art history to visual culture is marked by a shift in principles of coherence —from a history of style, or an analysis of form, to a genealogy of the subject.'[11]

NOTES
1. Mike Kelley, 'Missing Time: Works on Paper 1974– 1976, Reconsidered', in *Mike Kelley, Minor Histories: Statements, Conversations, Proposals*, ed. John C. Welchman (Cambridge: MIT Press, 2004), p.64.
2. Timothy Martin, 'Abuse and Composition: Notes on Missing Time', in *Mike Kelley 1985–1996*, ed. José Lebrero Stals (Barcelona: Museu d'Art Contemporani de Barcelona, 1997), p.84.
3. Edward Tufte, 'Ask E.T.: Design of causal diagrams: Barr art chart, Lombardi diagrams, evolutionary trees, Feynman diagrams, timelines', December 1, 2003, online at http://www.edwardtufte.com/ bboard/q-and-a-fetch-msg?msg_id=0000yO&topic_ id=1. See also, Tufte, *Beautiful Evidence* (Cheshire, CT: Graphics Press, 2006).
4. Mayer Schapiro, 'Nature of Abstract Art (1937)', in *Modern Art: 19th and 20th Centuries, selected papers* (New York: George Braziller, 1978), pp.187–88.
5. Robert Motherwell, 'The School of New York', preface to *Seventeen Modern American Painters* (1951), in *The Collected Writings of Robert Motherwell*, ed. Stephanie Terenzio (New York: Oxford University Press, 1992), p.83.
6. Max Horkheimer and Theodor Adorno, *The Dialectic of Enlightenment*, tr. John Cumming (New York: Continuum, 1989), pp.130–31.
7. Mike Kelley, 'Repressed Architectural Memory Replaced with Psychic Reality', in *ANY: Architecture New York*, no. 15 (1996), p.36.
8. Herbert Marcuse, 'The Obsolescence of the Freudian Concept of Man', in *Critical Theory and Society*, ed. Stephen Eric Bronner and Douglas MacKay Kellner (New York: Routledge, 1989), p.236.
9. Ibid., p.239.
10. Rosalind Krauss, 'Welcome to the Cultural Revolution', in *October* 77 (summer 1996), p.85.
11. Hal Foster, 'The Archive without Museums', in *October* 77 (summer 1996), p.103.

ARCHITECTURAL DESIG

October 1963   Price 4/-

lic on wood with steel frame, 101.5 × 115 × 3 inches
age courtesy Kelley Studio

WELCOM

Mike Kelley, *Entry Way (Genealogical Chart)* (1995), Acry
photograph by Fredrik Nilsen, in

Dust jacket of Richard Hamilton, *Collected Words* (London: Thames & Hudson, 1982)

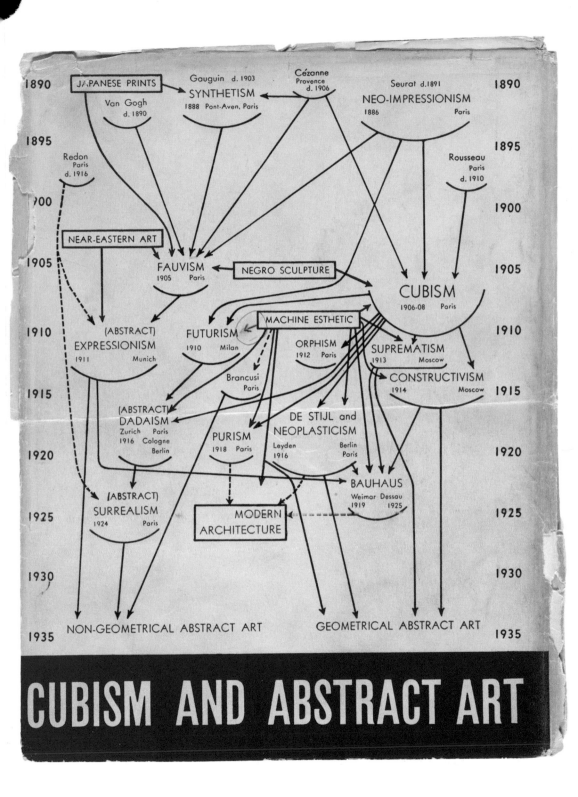

Alfred H. Barr, Cover of the exhibition catalogue *Cubism and Abstract Art* (New York: MoMA, 1936), $7\frac{3}{4} \times 10\frac{1}{4}$ inches
© The Museum of Modern Art Archives, New York

COLLECTED WORDS

By Rob Giampietro

AMES ROOM

cupants of an Ames Room appear to those
wing it from a peephole at a fixed point
be greatly distorted in size. Someone
y appear the size of a giant one moment,
d, crossing the room, seem no larger than
aby the next. In fact, it is the room that
listorted, not its occupants. Created in
46 by American opthamologist Adelbert
es, Jr., almost none of the walls or floors
an Ames Room are at right angles, even
ugh the room appears to be a perfect cube.
or and ceiling slope; one back corner is
ich farther away than the other. The room
ys on our predisposition to judge size
mparatively and gauge space according to
ed laws of perspective defined during the
naissance by Alberti and others. Richard
milton cites Ames's work in his book
llected Words alongside two reproductions
his early works, Induction study (1950)
d Chromatic spiral (1950). Next to this
nble of diagonal lines, both abstractly
miniscent of Collected Words's cover,
milton writes, Perspective is the dominant
e in our interpretation of any image.
e human eye will read diagonal marks
having spatial connotations even when
ey are contradicted by other clues.
e Ames experiment in which perspective
s so perverted as to propose a giant
man being in one corner and a midget in
other corner of a logical-seeming room
oved this convincingly.
    See also: Interior I

BICYCLE WHEEL (1913)

rcel Duchamp inverted the front wheel of
icycle wheel and attached it to an ordinary
ol for what has come to be called his first
dymade, though he did not officially coin
e term until 1915. The sculpture seems to
a celebration, at least to some degree, of
nt-less, going-in-circles kind of motion,
h Duchamp frequently comparing the
eel's spinning to 'flames dancing in a
place' or the back-and-forth of a game of
ess. Collected Words collects a number of
milton's writings about Duchamp, including
eneral piece on Duchamp he wrote for Art
ernational on the occasion of Duchamp's
rospective at the Pasadena Museum in
3, which mentions the Bicycle Wheel: [it] is
dence of Duchamp's concern with motion.
ve look for intention it seems to have
e significance other than as an enjoyable
memade toy. Hamilton goes on to point
that by appropriating objects as sculpture
her than making them himself, Duchamp
s able to satisfy the desire to suppress the
istic hand, leaving the mind in command.
e Bicycle Wheel appears on Collected
rds's back cover in a photograph that also
ludes Hamilton's own readymade-inspired
ce Epiphany (1964), his painting Interior I

(1964), and his screenprint homage A little of
Roy Lichtenstein for... (1964).
    See also: Sign

COLLAGE WITH SQUARES ARRANGED ACCORDING TO THE LAWS OF CHANCE (1916–17)

Collage, of course, was as important for Dada
artist Hans Arp as it was for Hamilton and
other Pop Artists. The critic John Elderfield
cites a story by Hans Richter, Arp's colleague,
who 'claim[ed] that the "law of chance" was
discovered when Arp tore up a failed drawing
and was struck by the pattern it made on the
floor.' Like Duchamp's readymade,
Arp's collage minimises the artist's hand
and supplants a logical chain of ideas with a
more automatic, spontaneous way of making.
There is a distinction made, too, between
accident (in the negative sense) and chance
(in the positive sense). Graphically, Arp's
collage is reminiscent of Theo van Doesburg
and Kurt Schwitters's 1922 invitation to a
Small Dada Evening (Kleine Dada Soirée), as
well as Hamilton's photograph of Duchamp's
unordered notes from the Green Box on p.194
of Collected Words and the cover of Collected
Words itself, with its tumbling sense of order
in a very disorderly desktop.
    See also: Green Box; 'Urbane Image'

DROSTE EFFECT

The Droste Effect is named for a brand of
Dutch cocoa whose box has a picture of a
nurse holding a serving tray with a cup of
hot chocolate and a box of the same brand
of cocoa bearing the image on the box. Since
the rendering of the nurse holding the tray is
relatively realistic, the Droste Effect is a Pop
play both on space and time. Theoretically,
on the smaller version of the box in the
picture is a still smaller version of the box
in the picture, and on and on into infinity. In
heraldry this shield-within-an-identical shield
is termed mise en abyme. The play on time
happens, whether on a shield or a cocoa box,
because the moment of unique description
coincides with an identical description's prior
existence. The inclusion of an exact copy,
then, creates both window through the surface
and a timeline into the past to when the
presumed 'original' was created. The effect
can be seen in Hamilton's painting Interior I,
where the entire painting itself is reproduced
on the far right edge of the painting. A photo
of Interior I appears within another photo on
Collected Words's back cover.
    See also: Interior I; X

EPIPHANY (1964)

Hamilton's Epiphany shares much in both
form and strategy with Duchamp's Bicycle
Wheel. Both are based on large circles—

Epiphany is slightly larger—and both are
'found' or readymade objects presented via
the artist in the gallery space to the public.
In a Guardian interview about his 'Imaging
Ulysses' show at the British Museum in 2002,
Hamilton compares James Joyce to Duchamp
and says, 'Their genius pervades my life'.
Hamilton argues that Joyce's concept of
epiphany, a moment of profound illumination
in which the soul of the commonest object
appears to us radiant, is uncannily parallel to
Duchamp's recognition of undistinguished
objects as full of an illimitable aesthetic
appeal. I sometimes wonder, Hamilton muses,
if a sudden epiphany hit Marcel Duchamp
when he picked up a bicycle wheel and put
it through a hole in the top of a kitchen stool
in 1913. I experienced such a moment of
understanding when I encountered a large
button in a seedy gift shop in Pacific Ocean
Park, Venice, California, with the words
SLIP IT TO ME blatantly displayed across
it. The greatly enlarged version which I
characterised as a work of art was entitled
Epiphany.
    Epiphany appears on Collected Words's
cover reproduced in black and white
with orange and blue blots of paint and is
considered one of Hamilton's first 'Products'.
    See also: Bicycle Wheel; Sign

FONTS

Hamilton espouses a certain amount of
typographic diversity both in his 'typotranslation' of Duchamp's notes for the
Green Box and in the settings of the essays
in Collected Words itself. In the 'Preamble'
to the book, he writes, Oddities of typesetting
in the later parts of the book relate the
sections back to their original publication,
or non-publication, and also to their subject
matter. A piece written for the Sunday
Times or The Times Educational Supplement
looks plausible set in Times Roman. An
unpublished text is likely to appear in more
intimate italics. A general lack of conformity
helps to isolate and identify segments
of a sporadic and diverse output (italics
Hamilton's). In addition to Times Roman,
Hamilton uses Helvetica for the majority
of essays. For this reason, in this glossary
Hamilton's direct quotations from the book
appear in Helvetica. Collected Words also
uses ITC Century Book for transcripts or
letters and Monotype Garamond for a single
essay from Design magazine. Plantin, Modern,
and Bembo are used in the discussion of
typesetting the Green Box, and Futura is
used in the collaborations with Dieter Roth.
Collected Words's front and back covers
include at least eight different typefaces in
their original contexts.
    See also: Green Box

GREEN BOX (1934)

Publishing under his nom de plume Rrose
Sélavy, Duchamp recreated '93 documents
(photographs, drawings, and manuscript notes
of the years 1911–1915) as well as a plate in
colour' with obsessive exactitude—down to
every last blot and tear—in a limited edition
of 300 green-felt–wrapped cardboard boxes
bearing the title of his great work, The Bride
stripped bare by her bachelors, even (aka The
Large Glass, 1915–23). The Green Box was
not meant to supplement the Large Glass but
to extend it into the verbal sphere. Hamilton
writes, [Duchamp] contrived an art form

without parallel, a unique marriage of visual and linguistic concepts. [...] The text exists beside the Glass as a commentary and within it as a necessary component of its structure. Without the notes the painting loses some of its significance and without the monumental presence of the Glass the notes have an air of random irrelevance.

Throughout 1959–60 Hamilton undertook a typographic English translation of the *Green Box* with Yale art history professor George Head Hamilton. Duchamp introduced the two men to one another. The professor handled the translation from French to English, and the artist handled the translation from facsimile to typography. The challenge, of course, was to ensure that [Duchamp's] doubts, the rethinks and doubletakes, the flat bewilderment and the moments of assurance; the pauses and reaffirmations are there, the winces, private sniggers, and nervous tics [when] calligraphy is converted into hard metal. Hamilton's rendition of the *Green Box* in book form also required sequencing the documents with his usual idiosyncratic thoughtfulness.

In 1966 Hamilton created a full-scale replica of the *Large Glass* for the Tate Gallery's retrospective when the original was considered too fragile to travel from the USA. In 2003 Hamilton used Adobe Illustrator to create *Typo/Topography*, in which the book's pages are unbound and superimposed onto a digital rendition of the *Large Glass* itself at actual size. The effect of these pages scattered over space is uncannily like that of the photograph of the contents of the *Green Box* itself on p.194 of *Collected Words*. The cover of *Collected Words*—which, like the *Green Box*, is a collection of artist's writings—shares this loose sense of visual organisation, although rather than translating the handmade to the mechanical as Duchamp does, Hamilton painstakingly illustrates several of the covers shown on top of a coarsely-screened photograph to create the cover image, working as he does in many of his collage paintings.

See also: *Collage with Squares...; Questions (from A–Z Box)*; *White Album*

HAMILTON, RICHARD

Hamilton shows himself reflected in a mirror for the poster of the 1982 Tate show 'Image and Process'. The image is identical to a 1974 project of Hamilton's entitled *Palindrome*. (A 'palindrome' is a phrase that reads the same backward or forward.) *Palindrome* was created at the invitation of art critic Nicholas Calas for a group edition of artist's multiples called 'Mirrors of the Mind' on the subject of mirrors. Hamilton's submission was created using stereoscopic lenticular printing, which involves interlacing strips from two two-dimensional images taken approximately two inches apart onto the back of plastic prism-like lenses. The result is a sense of three-dimensional depth without the special glasses. Hamilton writes, I touched the mirror surface and realised that the fact that I could see part of my physical self, as well as its reflection, made the visual experience stronger. [...] Reaching for a volume behind the mirror suggested that the use of three-dimensional photography might help to reconstruct that experience.

INTERIOR I (1964)

This painting started from Hamilton's fascination with a publicity still from the Douglas Sirk thriller *Shockproof* (1948) featuring the actress Patricia Knight in an oddly-lit and irregularly constructed living room, the body of a dead man at her feet. Knight stares slightly to the right of the viewer's glance though her body faces left, a positioning identical to that of the central figure of Velázquez's *Las Meninas* (1656), the Infanta Margarita, which Hamilton references in his essay on 'Interiors' in *Collected Words*: Velázquez's great interior painting Las Meninas must have been hanging around in my head waiting for some loving attention. (Picasso was obsessed with *Las Meninas*, too, completing 58 paintings inspired by it in 1957 alone.) Beyond the central figure of Knight, however, Hamilton was struck by the artifice of this particular interior image, shot by a wide-angle lens with walls that do not meet at right angles and multiple sources of lighting. Similar to an Ames Room, this film set had been constructed to fool the eye, deepening the flat, wide angle of the camera by imitating the rules of perspective. Despite these efforts, though, Hamilton writes that the foreground remained emphatically close and the recession extreme. In *Interior I*, the body has been removed, but the sense of disquiet remains because the perspectival ambiguity contributed more to the foreboding atmosphere than the casually observed body lying on the floor, partially concealed by a desk. In the process of making a collage, one whole is clipped and placed in a different whole. Contexts are changed, but resonances remain. What's been taken away affects what's there, and what's been brought together is altered by what's been left behind.

Hamilton connects his interiors to still lifes in an almost cinematic way, explaining that still life paintings [are], in a sense, interior details, as close-ups or 'insert' shots are in film. The cover of *Collected Words* can certainly be seen in this way, cropped from the desk of a larger room, perhaps even that of *Interior*, of which Hamilton made multiple versions. Also like the cover of *Collected Words*, *Interior I* combines painting on photo-reproduction, and this strategy, too, is discussed by Hamilton: I found that art was as often the subject as they were about rooms. [...] A secondary concern of my painting was this transformation of a work of art into a new image by the processing it receives through photography and printing and back again into painting. On *Collected Words*'s cover, *Interior I* is itself reproduced, selected, as it was, for the back cover image of an earlier printed publication of Hamilton's. Hamilton then photographed the back cover reproduction for the *Collected Words* cover image itself, heightening this photograph with his own drawing and painting. This 'original' altered photograph is then reproduced as the printed cover on the book itself. From reality to publicity still, reproduction to painting, painting to cover image, cover image to collage, and collage back to printed cover again: the result is a dizzying displacement not just of space but of time, each level stepped further back from reality toward representation, each reproduction altered slightly by the one that succeeds it.

See also: *Ames Room; Just what is it...*

JUST WHAT IS IT THAT MAKES TODAY'S HOMES SO DIFFERENT, SO APPEALING? (1956)

This small collage was submitted by John McHale, John Voelcker, and Hamilton fo the 'This Is Tomorrow' exhibition at Lond ICA. The image was also featured in the s catalog and posters. Heavily influenced b Eduardo Paolozzi's *Bunk* collages and lec from 1952, Hamilton famously describes image in *Collected Words* as tabular as we as pictorial. Included above this statemer a table of words from which the collage w supposedly developed.

In a virtuoso essay in the *New Left Rea* critic Hal Foster examines the implication of the term 'tabular' from almost every conceivable resonance. He begins, '"tabu derives from tabula, Latin for table, but a for writing-tablet, in which, in ancient us both painting and printing figure as mode of inscription.' Writing, then, is bound up with image-making, and vice versa, both for Hamilton and for the Pop Culture he investigates. Foster continues, 'his pictu register the traces of the visual-verbal hy characteristic of the magazine spread or tabloid layout (perhaps "tabular" connot "tabloid" as well), a hybrid that anticipat the visual-verbal sign (call it a bit or a by that dominates electronic media space to Foster points out that 'tabulation' is also systematic process favored by electronic media. He uses this systematisaton to correlate Hamilton's diversity of imagery with the techniques favoured by Madison Avenue itself: 'Like an ad-man, then, Ham tabulates—as in correlates—different media and messages, and tabulates—as i calculates—this correlation in terms of v appeal and psychological effect.' In Foste description, the spreadsheet almost appe before our eyes.

Foster then recalls that Hamilton car fully defined the collage as more than *me* tabular. It is also 'pictorial' in his formula a kind of hybrid in which the words becor types of pictures, arranged in many ways as words would be, within a square of wha Foster describes as 'semi-illusionistic spa and what Hamilton describes as 'domesti interiors', one of which is the site for *Just what is it...* What this creates is a rea that occurs not just in two dimensions bu in three, being translated and retranslate perpetually back-and-forth. Here Foster points out Walter Benjamin's assertion th in an age of mechanical reproduction, '"literacy" must include the decoding of captioned photographs.' From words to pictures, and back to words again.

Foster goes on, explaining that the ta image can function as a 'research model' for a new society. The laws that govern th society, written on tablets of course, sugg that Hamilton's tabular images are also 'p gogical investigations of a "new body of l a new subjective inscription, a new symbo order, of Pop society.' The tabular pictur not just evocative of a cluttered contemp magazine layout, it is also evocative of a cluttered shop window. Behind the glass an anthology of 'presentation techniques that 'mimes the distracted attention of th desirous viewer-consumer.' Our wanderi eyes are given much more wandering to d Pleasure, both sexual and consumptive, is the intended and eventual result.

The glass of the shop window is of course connected with the *Glass* of Duchamp, and ... many ways Duchamp's *Large Glass* is, for ... oth Foster and Hamilton, a 'proto-tabular' ... ork. But Foster explains what Hamilton ... nly intuits, which is that for this new tabular ... trategy to work it must tap not only into the ... ture, but also into the past. The effect of ... is disguise is, finally, to create a tableau, ... nd this final bit of tabular transmogrification ... ncludes Foster's essay. He writes, 'The ... bleau and the tabular can no longer be ... ld apart as distinctive forms. [...] This is ... nother Pop insight that Hamilton shares with ... chtenstein in particular: that today, in both ... mpositional order and subjective effect, ... ere is often no great difference between ... good comic or ad and a grand painting.'

Hamilton concludes the book with ... statement explicitly connecting his ... intings to the art of the past: I have never ... ade a painting which does not show an ... tense awareness of the human figure. ... llowing that he includes, on p.275, a ... able of Contents'. Its placement suggests ... s not there for navigation. It's almost an ... terthought. If Hamilton took away the cover ... llage, however, his readers would certainly ... lost. Like the tabular image *Just what* ... it...', the table was useful in the image's ... aking, but it is scarcely necessary for the ... age's reading.

See also: *Newspapers*; *Telephone*

KITAJ, R.B.

amilton mentions this British Pop artist in ... ssing when discussing his own painting ... n-up (1961). Hamilton writes, R.B. Kitaj is ... ble to assemble disconcertingly disparate ... yles in his paintings (an extreme case is ... ertain forms of Association Neglected ... efore). He has said of these jumps that they ... e, among other things, 'a change of pace'.

See also: *'Urbane Image'*

LE JOURNAL

casso's masterpiece of synthetic cubism ... ill *Life with Violin and Fruit* includes ... tual portions of the newspaper *Le Journal* ... om 6 and 9 December 1912 pasted to the ... ustration board. The newsprint is used ... stractly to create a bowl shape for the ... uit, decoratively to dress the table's skirt ... d the wallpapering behind the violin, ... presentationally via the masthead clipping ... show the newspaper lying on the table, ... d literally as the thing itself.

See also: *Newspapers*; *Telephone*

MUSEUM

roughout 1965–66, Hamilton made a ... ries of drawings, paintings, collages, ... d relief sculptures of Frank Lloyd ... right's Guggenheim Museum. Each is titled ... e *Solomon R. Guggenheim* with the word ... useum' conspicuously omitted. Hamilton ... ds it, instead, by cycling through a wide ... ray of visual styles that include and ... mic those found inside a museum like ... e Guggenheim itself: the architectural ... ndering, the Pop serial screenprint, the ... ntimental watercolour, even the ancient ... rm of bas relief. Though he omits the word ... useum' from the titles of these works, ... e word crops up elsewhere in *Collected* ... *rds* during his discussion of the domestic ... teriors that inform *Interior I*. He describes ... em as a set of anachronisms, a museum,

with the lingering residues of decorative styles that an inhabited space collects. Banal or beautiful, exquisite or sordid, each says a lot about its owner and something about humanity in general.

The Solomon R. Guggenheim—Architect's Visual, which is in the permanent collection of MoMA, is shown on a back cover on the back cover of *Collected Words*.

NEWSPAPERS

Newspapers is one of the words in the table Hamilton used to develop the collage *Just what is it...* This table also includes the words Man, Woman, Humanity, History, Food, Cinema, TV, Telephone, Comics (picture information), Words (textual information), Tape recording (aural information), Cars, Domestic appliances and Space. A newspaper, reproduced at an angle, is shown on the arm of a chair in the corner of the collage.

See also: *Just what is it...*; *Le Journal*

OBRIST, HANS-ULRICH

An influential Swiss curator and art critic currently co-directing the Serpentine Gallery in London. Interviewing Hamilton for *Tate Magazine* in 2003, Obrist asked him about *an Exhibit*, an exhibition staged by Hamilton with Victor Pasmore in 1957. Hamilton explained, Victor Pasmore told me that he liked the 'Man, Machine and Motion' show but didn't care for the pictures. He'd have preferred the show without a subject. Hamilton devised a show with no visual content beyond the division of space. Photographs included in *Collected Words* show acrylic panels of varying sizes and degrees of translucency intersecting in space at a different angles and depths. These overlapping planes are reminiscent of the depiction of printed matter on *Collected Words*'s cover. In the Obrist interview, Hamilton continues, I thought about what was novel in this experience of 'exhibition' and decided that it is a form that requires the movement of the spectator in a space. There are other ways to absorb information: watching a projected image in a cinema, reading a book; but an exhibition presents information in such a way that you are required to move to it rather than have it directed at you. [...] *an Exhibit* had no subject, no theme other than itself; it was self-referential.

See also: *Ames Room*

PEOPLE (1965–66)

The people in Hamilton's series *People* are an abstracted set of bathers blown up —Antonioni's *Blowup* is from 1966 as well —from a postcard image taken at Whitley Bay in northern England. The image yielded several variations, a medium-sized painting, a print on a photographic base, a postcard, a one-off 'multiple', and the cover for the March 1969 issue of *Studio International*. The *Studio International* cover is recreated in watercolour by Hamilton for the front cover of *Collected Words*.

Hamilton goes on, Photographs such as this [...] show a random sample of humanity. When broken down and analyzed they can provide an incredible amount of information about individuals and their activity. There is, however, a breaking-point, a stage at which the emulsion is too large to absorb the imprint of form. It was a search

for this moment of loss that became the real subject of the series. Photographers also refer to the amount of 'information' present on the photographic negative. When a print is overdeveloped, underexposed, or otherwise misprocessed, the result can muddy the mottling of a shadow or blow out a brightly-lit face. In this sense, Hamilton's photographed beachgoers face a double loss: their behaviours are gone, but so are their formal attributes, as there is simply not enough photographic information available on the negative to read their forms at such a high degree of enlargement. It is telling that Hamilton has not represented individuals in *People*; the very title suggests a multiple, or mass, number. As we learn less about these single human beings, we learn more about the specific photographic surface that's captured and grouped them.

See also: *Telephone*

QUESTIONS (FROM A–Z BOX) (1969)

The same year Hamilton wrote the essay 'Urbane Image' and its accompanying glossary for *Living Arts* 2, his fellow artist Joe Tilson was finishing a glossary-like, multi-authored collage work entitled *A–Z Box of Friends and Family*, and Hamilton was asked to be a part of the project. (The timing is uncanny —it's hard to imagine both artists weren't influenced in some way by Duchamp's *Green Box*, as Hamilton's 'typotranslation' had been published in 1960.) In his essay on *AAH!* (1962) in *Collected Words*, Hamilton describes Tilson's piece: The vertical panels were installed in rows running from A to Z. Various friends were selected either by surname or Christian name or initial. I was allocated 'R' for Richard but I liked the idea of 'R' for AAH! [... But] Joe didn't like undoing his picture every time I wanted my piece for a retrospective so I made a replica for my own use. Tilson made several contributions, one of which was the box itself, a dead ringer for a printer's California Job Case. Another of Tilson's contributions was a graphic for the letter Q, whose box includes a playfully drawn question mark.

The question mark returns in Tilson's 1969 follow-up *A–Z Box*, which extends ideas from the 1963 version, though all prints are now by Tilson himself. The letter Q's print, *Questions*, shows an image of the Great Sphinx of Giza screened in red on pink paper with the phrase 'Q?' screened in black Helvetica centered along the top edge. In one of two alterations to the source image, Tilson has superimposed Greta Garbo's face onto the Sphinx. The swap is classic Pop, exchanging a symbolic work from antiquity for an iconic star of the silver screen, but Tilson's work is particularly knowing. Following her work in the film *Mata Hari* (1931), Garbo became known as 'The Swedish Sphinx', an epithet that acknowledged both the widespread exoticism (triggered in part by the release of *Mata Hari*) and Garbo's visual transformation, aided by photographers like Edward Steichen and Clarence Bull from chubby extra to 'the most beautiful woman that ever lived' (at least according to the 1954 *Guinness Book of World Records*). 'Mata Hari' is the Indonesian term for the sun, literally translating to 'eye of the day'. The Egyptian Pharaoh whose image Garbo's character replaces is Kafra, or Kaf-Ra, which means 'Appearing like Ra', the Egyptian god whose eye was believed to be the sun. 'Kafra' may also be spelled 'Kafre', which is the name for a computer encryption method known as a 'block cypher' developed by researchers at Xerox's Palo Alto Research Center in 1989. The Kafre cypher relies on numerical constants from the RAND Corporation's famous 1955 book *A Million Random Digits with 100,000 Normal Deviates*, described by tech historian Tom Jennings as 'a monstrous anti-table, a work of intentional disorder produced by machine in an undoing of order itself' and 'guaranteed to contain absolutely no information' whatsoever. In other words, a higher form of chance.

The word 'sphinx' comes from the Greek 'sphiggo', meaning 'to strangle', which was the fate of those who answered the Sphinx's famous riddle—'Which creature in the morning goes on four feet, at noon on two, and in the evening upon three?'—incorrectly. Oedipus famously cracked the code: the answer is 'man'.

The second of Tilson's alterations is the creation of a moiré effect in which rays seem to emanate from Garbo's eyes. The effect, heightened by the pyramid in the background, is a reference to the 'all-seeing eye', or 'Eye of Providence', a Masonic symbol that appears most famously floating above an unfinished pyramid on the back of a US $1 bill.

See also: *'Urbane Image'*; *Green Box*

RADIO

The eye peering out from the spine of *Collected Words* belongs to part of a table Hamilton and collaborators John McHale and John Voelcker created for the spiral-bound *This Is Tomorrow* exhibition catalog. The table is titled 'One Chassis: Four Tools', and, in addition to the eye, it shows cropped images of an ear and skin from the hand and face. On the left are a series of frequencies ranging from zero to ∞ on a CPS, or cycles per second, scale. (CPS, once a common unit of frequency, was replaced by the hertz in 1960 shortly after *This Is Tomorrow* débuted.) These frequencies are divided among a set of horizontal bands beginning with 'skin pressure' at the bottom and 'cosmic rays' at the top. In the band from 10^4 to 10^{12} CPS is 'radio', here referring to the type of wave. 'Radio' is also described as a technology, along with television and photography, on the black vertical bar furthest to the right of the table. In keeping with organiser Theo Crosby's theme of habitation and the human senses, the table integrates key ideas about media and communication from Marshall McLuhan with ideas about systems and cybernetics from Norbert Wiener, both of whose ideas were then gaining prominence.

SIGN (1975)

Hamilton's 'Products' build on the ideas introduced with Duchamp's readymades, but they are particular to a Pop sensibility and high-gloss aesthetic. *Sign* is one of the first Products produced and is shown, presumably on the cover of a catalogue, bleeding off the bottom of *Collected Words*'s cover. Though it is perhaps the most prominent work by Hamilton on the cover, it is not discussed inside the book. To create it, Hamilton appropriated the logo for Ricard, a French brand of anise-flavoured liqueur, intervening only to add an 'H' in order to spell his first name. As such, *Sign* both names and misnames; it is at once

a sign for someone and an altered sign for something else, anticipating efforts at 'culture jamming' by two decades or more. Hamilton's final *Sign*, made with vitreous enamel on steel, is nearly identical to a real Ricard sign that would be posted on the wall of a bar or café. These original Ricard signs go up for auction on eBay all the time. One description reads: 'Ricard Anisette Liquor is found on the tables at all the European cafés. Bright advertising letters of in red, yellow, and blue. Excellent condition. This is original, and bought in France. You may feel like you are at a wonderful café in Paris. Thanks for looking, and good luck!'

See also: *Bicycle Wheel*

TELEPHONE

Hamilton is interested in electronic communication media of all types, but certainly the telephone ranks high on the list, appearing in the hand of a young woman on the television screen of *Just what is it…*, in the art-directed cover photograph for *Living Arts 2* and its accompanying essay 'Urbane Image', and in the art directions relayed to Ed Paschke in Chicago for the exhibition *Art by Telephone* in 1969. The *Living Arts 2* cover is recreated in watercolour for *Collected Words*'s cover, although Bell's 'Princess' model telephone is obscured by the *Studio* magazine cover featuring *People*. Hamilton discusses the telephone in 'Urbane Image' this way: This month's playmate, however, is Miss June. […] She's built (37, 22, 36), sociable (show a record player and a couple of highballs), intelligent (use a record sleeve with Zen in the title), available through the Bell system (Princess handset), and has friendly eyes that come out green on Ektachrome.

The two paintings created by Hamilton and Ed Paschke, called *Chicago Project I* and *II*, blurred lines between the performative aspects of Fluxus and the photo enlargements of Pop painting as well as between the Conceptual Art instructions of Baldessari and Lewitt and the art direction and Young and Rubicam. Hamilton's script for 'Composition', included on p. 268 of *Collected Words*, begins by asking Paschke to Get a coloured postcard in the Chicago area of a subject in Chicago and proceeds, almost clinically, through Leave 20% of the surface untouched, black and white, to conclude: Either use transparent stains or opaque colours, some thick, some thin, which areas are at your discretion. There is some agency yielded to the maker and some instruction provided by the conceiver. The telephone links brain and hand, mind and body, like a cybernetic version of the nervous system.

The Tate's educational website offers a similar strategy to young students of art first learning about Cubism. 'The difference between a perspective and a Cubist representation of reality,' the site explains, 'can be compared to the way two people might describe the same scene to us on the telephone. […] The first person gives us a steady mental picture. But the second person's description is lively and becomes increasingly revealing as we mentally assemble the various pieces of information they give us.'

See also: *Just what is it…*; *Le Journal*; *People*; *'Urbane Image'*

'URBANE IMAGE'

Hamilton wrote what is probably his best-known essay as part of a package for the ICA's *Living Arts* magazine in 1963. The te… of the essay is a rapid-fire collage of Pop culture signifiers that begins, Chrysler Vice-President Virgil Exner models the ple… detailing of the sleek 'flight sweep'—linin… the crustacean recesses of Plymouth's headlamp hood with mirror-like chrome, a… continues breathlessly from there. Hamilt… was certainly not alone in these text-collag… explorations. Around the same time, fellow… Pop artist Eduardo Paolozzi constructed h… novel *Kex* from bits of dimestore thrillers, reviews, and magazine ads; artist Tom Phil… discovered a used copy of W.H. Mallock's 1892 novel *A Human Document* by chance… a walk with R.B. Kitaj and began altering it… his collage novel *A Humument*; Graham R… strung phrases from women's magazines together to create the 437-page story *Woman's World*; and William Burroughs w… actively experimenting with and promotin… 'cut-up' technique in the USA. Preceding a… informing these mid-1960s efforts were D… founder Tristan Tzara's poem created fro… words drawn randomly from a hat in the 1… and T.S. Eliot's 'The Waste Land' from 192… Eliot's poem, in particular, seems a useful… template for 'Urbane Image', as it conclude… with a lengthy set of explanatory endnotes… Hamilton dubs his endnotes a 'Glossary' w… begins with *Virgil Exner*—Chief body styli… for the Chrysler Corporation from 1953 u… 1961—and concludes with *Affirmative*—Ye… Somewhat forced expression of need to conclude on a grandly positive rhetorical note.

In an interview with Michael Compton… for *Audio Arts* magazine in 1983 just after… *Collected Words* came out, Hamilton discu… 'Urbane Image' at length as a turning poin…

I produced a very serious piece of w… trying to express what I had been doing i… painting. And I used collage, pastiche, an… all the other devices that were applicable… to paintings, which seemed to be easily converted to the written word. And within… a week of that being published I met Eric… Brausen in the gallery on Bond Street: 'Say, what about coming up to Highgate'… And she said, 'Well, I won't bother comin… up to Highgate but I saw that piece in the… magazine and let's fix up a show.' […] It struck me then that the power of the w… is greater than the power of the brush.

He continues:
Having written about things in a way that makes people think they're serious and reasoned, I had almost come to the conclusion that perhaps the paintings we… reasoned and serious. And it takes a long… time before the thought begins to come back that maybe you don't know what ye… doing. And now I'm thoroughly convince… that I don't know what I'm doing and tha… writing is a way of finding out. Very often… the writing occurs after the event or part… through it. It's not like writing a program, although I have done that. Understandin… begins to come back to the work from th… need to think about it.

With photographer Robert Freeman, Hamilton created a wraparound front and… back cover for *Living Arts 2* to complemen… his essay. The cover image—an oversized… still life that includes many of the objects amilton discusses—provides another, ore visual kind of glossary. Hamilton as reproduced the *Living Arts 2* cover a watercolour on the cover of *Collected ords*.

See also: *Collage with Squares…*; *itaj, R.B.*; *Questions (from A–Z Box)*; *elephone*

Rod van Uchelen
P·A·S·T·E·-·U·P
Production Techniques and New Applications

VAN UCHELEN, ROD

ollected Words was designed and produced sing a layout method known as 'paste-p'—sort of a commercial artist's version of ollage—and *Collected Words*'s cover bears ore than a passing resemblance to the elf-reflexive cover of designer Rod van chelen's 1978 primer on the subject, *aste-Up*. (The two books are also identical a size and internal layout and typesetting.) he paste-up method, van Uchelen writes a the introduction, is simple but essential: t's like learning to use to use the typewriter.' amilton was certainly aware of it, and, ecause of past difficulties, very hands-on y the time of *Collected Words*. In his note o 'An exposition of *$he*', Hamilton writes, its text was edited for its first publication –cuts have been replaced. A paragraph as pasted up incorrectly at the layout tage, that error is corrected. The earlier ersion of the essay Hamilton refers to ppeared in Theo Crosby's *Architectural esign* in October 1962, the cover of which s shown toward the top of the back cover of *ollected Words*. In *Paste-Up*, van Uchelen arns editors and paste-up artists against rrors of this sort: 'Once it is with the latemaker, mistakes are costly to correct. he content of a paste-up is usually not the rtist's responsibility, but the sizing and raphic reproduction are.'

Hamilton's interest in paste-up methods as more than simply technical, however. oward the end of the essay he observes, he ad for the Westinghouse vacuum cleaner emonstrates an endearing characteristic f modern visual technique which I have een at pains to exploit—the overlapping f presentation styles and methods. hotograph becomes diagram, diagram ows into text. This casual adhesion of isparate conventions has always been a actor in my paintings.

See also: *Droste Effect*; *X*

WHITE ALBUM

aul McCartney and Hamilton worked losely together to design both the cover of he album and a poster insert slipped into he double-disc set of the Beatles' ninth lbum, officially called *The Beatles* (1968) ut known informally as the 'White Album'.

While it's likely that the 'White Album' is included on the cover of *Collected Words*, it is also almost impossible to prove. Hamilton does explain the genesis of the project on p.105: Robert Frasier, my swinging art dealer, was friendly not only with Mick Jagger and the Stones but also with the Beatles. Hamilton explains that he was drawn to the job both because of the power of the Beatles and the size of the edition, potentially in the region of 5,000,000, a mass scale that suited Hamilton's popular sensibilities, the ultimate multiple image, as far as numbers were concerned. The twist, then, was how to make such a mass-produced object feel rare, and Hamilton staked his whole design on achieving this effect: I suggested a plain white cover so pure that it would seem to place it in the context of the most esoteric art publications. To further this ambiguity, I took it more into the little press field by individually numbering each cover.

The poster insert was where Hamilton spent the majority of his design time. He selected a sampling of personal photos from the Beatles and created a collage only slightly more controlled in feel than if the photos were to be strewn across a tabletop. He explains his process: Because the sheet was folded three times to bring it to the square shape for insertion into the album, the composition was interestingly complicated by the need to consider it as a series of subsidiary compositions. The top right and left hand square are front and back of the folder and had to stand independently as well as be a double spread together. *Collected Words*'s front and back covers are conceived in exactly the same way.

See also: *Green Box*

X

Hamilton's painting and corresponding screenprint *My Marilyn* (1965)—sometimes credited as *My Marilyn (paste-up)*—appropriates contact sheets from a photoshoot by George Barris for *Town* magazine showing Marilyn Monroe at the beach. The contact sheets, released after Monroe's death, carry her markings and edits: the star routinely demanded photo approval before publication. Hamilton explains, She made indications, brutally and beautifully in conflict with the image […] crosses and ticks, notes for retouching, instructions to the photographer, even the venting of physical aggression by attacking the emulsion with nail-file or scissors. Of particular interest to Hamilton were Monroe's 'X' marks, recreated fastidiously both in paint and screened ink. Hamilton notes their ambiguity: There is a fortuitous narcissism to be seen for the negating cross is also the childish symbol for a kiss. The X is a contradictory symbol; while Monroe meant her Xs as a rejection, the mark's cultural meanings also include both the lover's kiss and the treasure's home. Monroe hated, was loved, and Hamilton strikes gold in the process.

My Marilyn shares a great deal compositionally with Hamilton's poster insert for The Beatles, which is also a collage of publicity images and personal stills. *My Marilyn*, dating three years earlier, is unlike previous pictures in that there is an avoidance of a unifying perspective. The individual shots are spread across the panel like a comic strip, four photographs,

each represented three times on a different scale—perspective is respected only within each frame. *Collected Words*'s cover takes this perspectival jumble even further: each cover creates the frame-within-a-frame effect, but unlike *My Marilyn* these overlapping frames are shown in three dimensions rather than two. Several of the covers shown cross at oblique angles, a cascading series of invisible Xs tumbling through space, similar to his abstract 1950 compositions *Chromatic spiral* and *Induction study*.

See also: *Ames Room*; *Droste Effect*; *Van Uchelen, Rod*; *White Album*

YOUNG (AIMED AT YOUTH)

One of the terms on Hamilton's table titled 'Pop Art Is:' from a letter written to Alison and Peter Smithson, fellow members of the Independent Group, in January 1957 a few months after *This Is Tomorrow*. The table also includes the words Popular (designed for a mass audience), Transient (short-term solution), Expendible (easily forgotten), Low cost, Mass produced, Witty, Sexy, Gimmicky, Glamorous, and Big business. After his success with the 'tabular' painting *Just what is it…*, Hamilton advises this list is just the beginning. Perhaps the first part of our task is the analysis of Pop Art and the production of a table.

See also: *Just what is it…*; *Newspapers*

ZABO

An image of California bodybuilder Irvin 'Zabo' Koszewski was used by Hamilton as the 'Man' holding the Tootsie Pop in *Just what is it…*, though the choice of Zabo himself might be attributable to fellow *This Is Tomorrow* collaborator John McHale, who probably saw Zabo as part of Mae West's burlesque review when it passed through New Haven in the mid 1950s while McHale was studying art at Yale. Winner of 'Mr California' titles in 1953 and 1954, and a fair-weather Hollywood star of stage and screen, Zabo received the World Gym Lifetime Achievement Award in 2006 and commemorated the honor by giving over 3,000 of his personal photographs to *Graphic Muscle* magazine, which published them throughout the year. According to *Graphic Muscle*, 'Zabo was immortalised in 1956 by British Pop artist David [sic] Hamilton' as part of 'one of the landmark images in the history of art.'

See also: *Just what is it…*

The Aesthetics of Distribution (3)

RIGHT TO BURN

A drink with Christoph Keller
by Stuart Bailey and Sarah Crowner

Transcribed from a late night recording on
Christoph's farm Stählemühle, close to Lake
Constance in rural Germany, May 2007.

A bottle is opened

Christoph Keller: Let's start with something easy.
This is a schnaps made from the Black Forest
Cherry, which is actually a trademark like Whisky
or Champagne, meaning you can't call it Black
Forest Cherry if the fruit isn't actually from the
Black Forest and distilled within the vicinity.
I buy them from an organic farmer who lives in
one of those incredible valleys which fluctuate
between 200 and 1600 metres, all very dark woods
with places where you can't see any light because
it's so densely forested.

Schwarzwälder Kirschwasser is poured

CK: He has a farm with maybe 30 hectares
of cherry trees and machines which hold the
trees and shape them. There are huge nets to
catch the fruit when it falls, and a kind of
giant vacuum cleaner which sucks them all in.
There are so many trees—around 4000 I think—
that it's impossible to harvest them in any other
way. The fruit used for distilling is not comparable
to normal fruit, because it's not grown to be eaten,
but to be left on the trees as long as possible to
get the fullest flavour. It then has to be harvested
very quickly just before the rotting starts, when
they contain the most sugar and strongest aroma.

All: Cheers. [*clink*]

CK: This is also our silver medal winner [*laughs*]
in the biggest European schnaps event, which is
some kind of cross between the Olympic Games
and Documenta.

Stuart Bailey: And does winning that prize mean
you've stopped thinking of yourself as a dilettante
distiller?

CK: Well, I still believe in the dilettante as a kind
of *leifmotiv*, but obviously if you do something
very enthusiastically—even as a dilettante-
enthusiast—at some point you produce quality
that is so-called professional. Then again, perhaps
it doesn't really apply because we're working in
very small quantities here, maybe 200 bottles.
A professional distiller makes more like 1000
litres or 2000 bottles, in which case it's far more
difficult to maintain the same quality. But no …
in my mind at least it's still a dilettante hobby.

SB: I presume that you started the art publishing
house Revolver as a dilettante too. As you know,
I'm interested in the idea of maintaining a state of
permanent dilettantism …

Sarah Crowner: Do you prefer that to the idea of
the professional?

CK: I'm not actually sure I necessarily *prefer* it,
as such—I'm just *like that*. As a kid I always did
as much stuff as possible … I tried all the sports,
all the musical instruments, played around a lot,
but at some point always fell off. I never had the
guts to keep going through the crisis points, and
this was also true of the publishing. That's very
negative, but on the positive side, I'm also very
interested in that underlying Renaissance idea
—of universal man, scientist, whatever—which
has completely changed since digital media.
 Now *studium generale* or whatever you want
to call it, is so much easier because previously,
even before you could research, you had to
research *how* to research—which bibliographies
to use, which libraries, and so on, so this is really
a landmark. Of course, we also know all the side-
effects too—of information being dubiously edited
and controlled, and so on, but still the implication
is there. With digital media this universal science
is increasingly possible, and as a consequence I
think I'm personally getting more dilettante every
year.
 The reason I became a publisher, though, was
actually through a baseball club which I started

at the end of the 1980s after I was an exchange student at a high school in New Jersey. I was fascinated with the sport and so started a team in my hometown near Stuttgart called the Leonberg Lobsters.

Laughter

CK: Then the big question was how to design the uniform, the logo for the cap ...

SB: ... and the lobster claw was the baseball mitt.

CK: Of course, of course! And that's how I started to work with the early Corel Draw software—simply because someone had to do it. I found it quite simple and interesting, and I kept on designing stuff for baseball. Later I even made stuff for the Major League Baseball organisation to make a living while I was studying art and art history.

SB: That's odd ... I also became involved in a similar way through second-hand American sports. I was in provincial English teams with that same sense of being at least as interested in the badge and the uniform as the sport —not completely, but I think as equally as the game itself.

CK: The physical aesthetic is very much an aspect and an attraction of all the American sports— much more so than soccer, for instance.

SB: Traditionally, yes, but don't you think the European aesthetic is inevitably going the same way?—inevitable in the sense of society generally approximating American models. I mean, consider the last decade of soccer kits ... and international cricket is even more extreme, from the completely white, traditionally neutral non-uniform, to the current vogue for vivid colours.

CK: I only know the soccer ones, to be honest, and they just get worse and worse. Sometimes you see a nicely made one but the turnaround is so fast that they never get established. Jack Daniels was sponsoring St. Pauli the other year, and their shirt was brown with stripes—it was a really beautiful thing, but that was definitely an exception. At the moment Adidas is taking over everything, so they all have these stupid shirts with idiotic collars just to generate this year's fashion. We all know the

story—planned obsolescence is nothing new —but the results are always such crap. The American sports have a much more direct attention to the equipment and fashion, though. What was your local team called?

SB: The Selby Siclones ...

Laughter

SB: ... as in cyclone, whirlwind ... but the important thing was that it wasn't spelled C-Y but S-I for the visual alliteration.

CK: So it was SS ...

SB: Yes, and that's exactly the same point in terms of language, right?—that the aesthetic of the words is contrived in the same sport-specific way as the uniforms—and soccer teams are appropriately more mundane, so you get Manchester United or Sheffield Wednesday.

CK: Kids would never do anything so specifically American anymore because America is so out of fashion at the moment. As a European teenager growing up in the 1980s America was still a kind of Golden Land—you'd really aspire to go there, live there ... be an American, really ... and now it's changed completely. Not for our generation, but for today's teenagers. Anyway, back to the question: so I knew how to use Corel Draw ...

SB: ... and how to run a team ...

CK: Right, and the funny thing about my baseball career is that I started as a pitcher ...

SB: [*laughing*] ... and ended up designing the badge!

CK: [*laughing*] It's even worse! We won the championship for five consecutive years, so we kept moving up a one league each time. In the first year I was a pitcher, but by the second year I was already not good enough. In the third year we bought some people from South Africa to play for us, then I became an infielder, then an outfielder, and after that, because my hitting was also not good enough by this point, I became the announcer!—the guy with the microphone to explain to people what's happening on the field! That's what you call a downward spiral of dilettantism ...

72

Original
Schwarzwälder
KIRSCH
KIRSCHWASSER
Wasser

50 cl   42 %

Stählemühle
MÜNCHHÖF IM HEGAU

Deutsches Erzeugnis

Edelbrand aus Original Schwarzwälder
Süßkirschen aus dem Hesselbacher Tal.
In Abfindung nach altem Rezept gebrannt.

C K\ 06.1
J *2006*

HEGAU-BRENNEREI STÄHLEMÜHLE, 78253 EIGELTINGEN-MÜNCHHÖF
SCHOELLER & KELLER, WWW.STAEHLEMUEHLE.DE

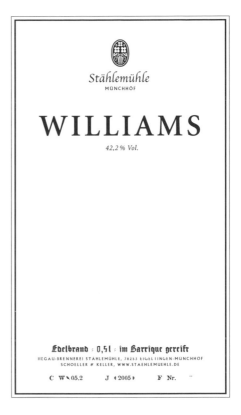

Stählemühle
MÜNCHHÖF

WILLIAMS

42,2 % Vol.

Edelbrand · 0,5 l · im Barrique gereift

HEGAU-BRENNEREI STÄHLEMÜHLE, 78253 EIGELTINGEN-MÜNCHHÖF
SCHOELLER & KELLER, WWW.STAEHLEMUEHLE.DE

C W\ 05.2   J *2005*   F Nr.

Ein Edelbrand aus aromatischen, vollreifen Williams-Christ Birnen aus den sonnenverwöhnten Obstanbaugebieten des nördlichen Bodensees. Als bäuerliches Erzeugnis nach uralter Brenn-Tradition schonend destilliert in der *Hegau-Brennerei Stählemühle*, Münchhöf. Nach der Reifung im Eichenfass von Hand abgefüllt in streng kontrollierter und limitierter Auflage. Spitzenbrand mit voller Fruchtnote.

Stählemühle
MÜNCHHÖF

Holder

42,2 % Vol.

Edelbrand · 0,5l · Deutsches Erzeugnis

HEGAU-BRENNEREI STÄHLEMÜHLE, 78253 EIGELTINGEN-MÜNCHHÖF
SCHOELLER UND KELLER, WWW.STAEHLEMUEHLE.DE

C HO 06.1   J ¢2006¢   F Nr.

Stählemühle
MÜNCHHÖF

ORIGINAL
·HEGAUER·
Quitten
· WASSER ·
44,4 % vol.
gebrannt aus vollreifen
Apfel- und Birnenquitten
Edelobstbrand
· 50 cl ·
Deutsches Erzeugnis

HEGAU-BRENNEREI STÄHLEMÜHLE, 78253 EIGELTINGEN-MÜNCHHÖF
SCHOELLER & KELLER, WWW.STAEHLEMUEHLE.DE

C HQ 06.1   J ¢2006¢   F Nr.

Die Früchte für unser Hegauer Quittenwasser setzen sich aus Apfelquitten, Birnenquitten und einem kleinen Anteil der seltenen Limonenquitten zusammen, werden sorgfältigst gereint und gemust und unter strengsten Kontrollen bei konstanter Temperatur vergoren. Der Aufwand lohnt sich, denn diesen edlen Brand dominiert ein feines, fruchtbetontes Spiel der typischen Quittenaromen. Die auffallende Eleganz am Gaumen bleibt in einem außergewöhnlich lang anhaltendem Abgang erhalten.

CK: Anyway, by this time in art school everyone would ask me to design—no, not design, to *make*—them cards or posters or whatever, and two good friends, the artist duo Korpys/Löffler approached me with a series of photographs they'd stolen from a police department which showed apartments used by the Red Army Faction during terrorist activities—bank robberies, kidnappings and so on. They were all completely camouflaged to look like normal 1970s German apartments—like something out of a Fassbinder film, completely zeitgeist. They always had these anterooms which were full of dynamite, walkie-talkies and weapons, which were obviously hidden away, but Korpys/Löffler were only interested in the anonymous ones, in the camouflage, how they did it, what the typical furniture was. They used the same technique the German police invented around the same time—some kind of computer-aided grid used to track terrorists—to find out where these objects in the apartments came from.

Anyway, I thought the material was incredible, suggested we should publish them, and they agreed. All I knew about books at this point was that we needed something called an ISBN number so people could order it. It turned out that it was very easy to become a publisher. You just paid twenty German marks at some kind of office for economic administration, and that was it—we could have as many ISBN numbers as we wanted. We printed their book in a edition of 300 copies on my laser printer, then bought an inkjet printer to do the colour plates [*laughs*]. It was a huge chaos of production as we were trying to print on both sides, then cut the pages from the sheets. We also had to devise a way of making a spine, as I had this idea—and still do, as a matter of fact—that a book is only a book if it has a spine.

We ended up binding it with the Socialist Union printer of Karlsrühe [*laughs*] who I suppose we felt closest to, and finally we called the publishing house Revolver because it fitted with the terrorism, but also the notion of a revolving

idea, as we intended to make other unknown things in the future.

SC: Did you end up selling the books? Was that even the point?

CK: We had absolutely no idea about selling. I had some idea about what was going on in art because I was working as an artist and with all those people, but I had no idea about books. I simply thought, we make these and sell them, then we do more. Ridiculous, but we had a lucky break when a friend of mine got some money from his parents who were trying to get rid of him. They gave him 30,000 Marks—which is quite cheap [*laughs*]—and after he lost a bit on the stock market I asked if he was interested in becoming a publisher, and he said, *oh, publisher, yeah, yeah, that sounds quite good.* He had nothing to do with art or books, in fact he was a musician.

It's a bit like that Bill Drummond story—he also calls himself a publisher when people ask him what he does, since he's not a musician anymore and he has this odd career. The title comes from when he was in the KLF and they wanted to rent a van but the guy at the rental told them you can't get a van if you call yourself a band, just say you're a publisher, so that's what he did. It's actually a good term for people like him, as it expresses any kind of work that has both aspects of being public and multiplied.

SB: And was it the same for you?

CK: Not exactly. The German term, 'Verlag', means something slightly different, because there's a distinct economic implication. It comes from a banking term, and means giving money to someone with the expectation of a profit —from *Verleihen*, to loan—but my friend liked the idea of the title, to be something without knowing anything about it. That's something common to most book publishers: you don't have to know anything, you don't have to have any abilities.

SB: I just had a similar experience making a book in perhaps the most autonomous situation you could imagine: a collaboration with an artist where neither the various galleries who paid for it, nor the museum that organised it, nor the publishers who are to distribute it, had any practical involvement with the book whatsoever—none of them even saw it up until it was printed and bound, other than to check their names on the cover … but you can be sure on the day it's sent to print there's suddenly a whole discussion and jostling about who's called what—the editor, the publisher, and the distributor … in that order of prestige. Of course all the words have slightly different meanings in different countries and languages, so the negotiation is very tricky. In the end the solution was agreed upon based on the Museum being called 'the producer' in the film industry sense, as distinct from 'the director'.

CK: And the publisher would be the equivalent to the film studio—MGM or Warners. Personally speaking, in the books I've been involved in, I always want to be called the publisher because even if I don't invest the money it's still an investment of time and work. I still put the *risk* into it.

SB: What does it means exactly—to publish now, in 2007? … I mean, if one party asks another 'to publish' what exactly is expected? Money? A distribution network? Some form of caretaking, organising, enforcement of standards, proofreading … or something else? I like the idea that 'risk' is the best answer. The book I mentioned previously is an example from the cusp of this wave of ambivalence where no-one really understands what the precise roles are anymore, everything's up for grabs and everyone naturally wants to claim the best labels while doing the least amount of work.

   In the end, of course, the real caretaking —I mean very literally taking care, worrying about a project, a book, rather than 'organising' in a more abstract sense, defaults to the end of the food chain where the genuine interest—or love, really—is. This is a gross generalisation, perhaps, but surely rings true to anyone involved in arts publishing at the moment. It's an extreme shift, and one which goes largely unchecked.

CK: Yes, and also in the last twenty or thirty years there's a related shift from the publisher being the one who invests, to the whole setup of arts publishing in Europe being subventioned, so it's always state or public money. That's the big difference with the U.S., because every book that is made in the art world in Europe is, in one way or another, subventioned by whatever trickle-down effect through the various institutions —publishers, galleries, museums, et cetera—with public money. Never directly, of course, and no-one would ever admit it too explicitly.

In the case of Revolver, we started with that friend's 30,000 Marks, and made eight books with artists we liked in the first year. We had to do it cheaply, of course, but that stage was paradise … we didn't sell anything and suddenly the money was gone, so we had to change the whole idea, at which point I started to collaborate with institutions. Because they're all subventioned, however, the nature of the funding directly influences the kinds of books that then get commissioned, the types of artists and subjects. Ultimately if you work for them it sounds like you have a job, but really you're just part of a system to keep people off the street! In this sense it's crazy, it's a problem, but on the other hand, without that money there wouldn't be a single book on art … or at least a small book would cost maybe 120 Euros if calculated it in direct relation to actual costs.

SB: Why weren't you selling those early books —because they weren't being distributed effectively or because no-one wanted them regardless of that?

CK: Well, the idea was to work with really young artists. My idea of the artist's book was largely Fluxus- and Ed Ruscha-inspired, with the idea of reviving the publication of art in the form of books, outside the usual channels of galleries and other institutions. At that time nobody cared for the people I was working with—Jonathan Monk, Franz Ackermann, Daniel Roth, or Christian Jankowski—so we'd go to art fairs trying to sell the books by hand … and that's the story of how it didn't work! Pretty soon we decided to go with a regular distributor, which as you know means you rarely get paid, and even if you do it's with incredible margins of something like 60-40% in their favour. Like everyone else, we did it anyway.

   One of the audiences we were always aiming at was our generation—meaning students or recent students who might have a little money from time to time to afford a book, but we found out they just don't exist, so neither site-specific selling nor regular distribution worked, and that was the point where we simply had to discount them. This carried on even up to the last year of Revolver, before I sold it: at that point we had a turnover of half a million Marks, but still only 10% of that was from selling books—the rest was from production services, design services, and suchlike, which had grown up around the publishing. That's how it works with art books—it has absolutely nothing to do with selling. Nothing.

SB: So essentially you're making your own work, creating jobs for yourself and your circle; by which I mean to say the essential outcome isn't the product, isn't the books, but rather the creation of 'work for Revolver'—a kind of backwards industry, perhaps even inverse capitalism, in the sense that it's about creating jobs rather than products.

CK: Yes, that's true, but of course in our case the end result *is* also important because, firstly, they generally *are* things we're interested in rather than a randomly desired or marketable product, and secondly because the collective result of those products is to create an aura around the company. All the products have to be good even though they don't sell. On many occasions I've put money into books that I knew I wouldn't sell more than 20 copies—because they generate a certain idea or respect for what both the book and publishing house stands for.

SB: And who benefits?

CK: With Revolver we were interested in creating the *profile* of a publishing house, and actually I think this is the only thing an art publisher can really do today—construct a framework or context for an artist. So there are artists who say, quite specifically, *I want to be in the Phaidon monograph series*, and others who say, *I want to be in the most hip publishing house, or most chic magazine—that's where I belong*. That's why it's important to set up this profile, why the products have to be right, even if, ecologically and economically, they make no sense, because there's a sense of balancing the whole field.

Revolver was simply an attempt to counteract the existing situation, and I think we actually achieved that, more or less, by the time I bailed out. In my opinion all these big arts publishing houses today aren't really publishers at all, precisely because they don't take any risks—they don't put money in books at all, they only work with funding institutions. The only ones that sell anything in a meaningful way are Taschen, some Phaidon stuff, and a few obvious large scale catalogues. For the rest it's *only* about generating marketable contexts, even intellectual contexts, and though it's not necessarily what we like, it *does* generate a framework.

SB: What's next?

CK: A blackcurrant schnaps … which is very time-consuming to make, although they do it in Austria, for some reason. I found this guy on the north shore of Lake Constance who harvests blackcurrants for the Austrian distillers, so we tried making a schnaps with it too.

A bottle of Ribisl blackcurrant schnaps is opened and poured

Stählemühle

Ribisl

It has a very strong aroma. In my opinion, though, the smell is better than the taste with this one [*laughs*] … but it's still a bronze medal!

SC: The process of publishing seems to parallel that of distilling. Do you think of these bottles in the same way as the books?

CK: The big difference for me is that for all these years we were making books, inevitably giving them away to people, and the reaction is always, *oh yeah, yeah, nice, good … thanks* … and that's it. With a bottle of schnaps, on the other hand, people will literally tear it away from me, *I have to drink it! It's amazing! How can I get some! I'll buy a whole box!* … an immediate genuine reaction, which is completely rewarding. I keep joking about winning these medals which, of course, I don't take too seriously, but sometimes it's good to get some kind of objective opinion about what you're making. It's quite difficult to know for sure because my nose is not so elaborate—I can evaluate books a lot better than I can schnaps—so it's important. Being dilettantes doesn't stop us wanting to make schnaps at a very high level.

SB: But is that 'high level' equivalent to publishing with Revolver? … I mean, in relation to what you were saying about creating a context which doesn't exist already—a space, aura, position, community, or however you want to describe it.

CK: With the alcohol it's a bit different, because the traditions are already in place. Unless I made a completely new schnaps, which is virtually impossible, the only thing I can do is give it a new context, with regard to how we make it, then how we present it—to indicate signs of a science, or craft … of an alchemist tradition and the sheer *effort* involved. We use old techniques and believe in associated ideas of purity, anyway, so this way of working fits with the general interest in organic production of recent years—usually in relation to the production of fruit, the slow food movement and suchlike. The only thing I can try to do with the schnaps itself—outside of its presentation —is produce objective quality.

That's the big difference to the book, because if you want to read one of the art books I've published you have to have studied art history. If I gave any of these books to my farming neighbours they'd immediately ask, *how the hell do you make a living out of this?* They wouldn't understand it because they don't know about art.

SC: And you don't have to have an education in alcohol to get the schnaps.

CK: Exactly, you simply don't have to be an expert. Of course there *are* schnaps experts and it's good if they like it too, but ultimately it's about this immediacy of you being able to say, yes, I like this one, or no, I don't like that one so much. Both responses are fine—it's the visibility and immediacy of the reaction that matters that makes the difference.

SB: I guess it's similar to the immediacy of theatre or performance, as opposed to architecture or fine art, where you're working with and on people and emotions in realtime—you can sense the atmosphere, tell if it's going well. Also, with performance or alcohol, once it's done it's gone. The effect might linger, but the art itself is transient, remembered. It turns into a memory —and maybe a hangover.

CK: Although I don't like theatre so much for other reasons, I do think it's a more honest medium than art, which I always feel is so complicated. There's almost no chance to enjoy art on a very simple level anymore—maybe once in a hundred occasions—because most of it requires thinking about hierarchies and strategies: why is this here, how did it come together, who's the curator, why is he working

with him or her, blah blah blah. In a certain sense, theatre is simply about whether the audience is being entertained or not.

SC: Are you saying that theatre is essentially concerned with delivering a work to an audience where art is more … one on one?

CK: No … not one on one … because art can easily exist without spectators, without an audience, and often does. So it's more like one on no-one. But I do mean theatre is closer to entertainment. someone's telling a story and someone else is enjoying it, where art is so much more … well, what can you get from it today? Value, investment, fame …

SB: Surely more than that. Last year I heard a speaker deliver a bullet-point teleological history of conceptual art, and the manner of presentation was *Art's Greatest Hits*—incredibly condensed, but also arrogant and didactic … Ryman did this, then LeWitt did this, then Buren did this, and so on. Something very rich and complex was reduced to a cross between a relay race and the Eurovision song contest.

Later on another speaker thankfully contested the violence of this presentation: the point isn't that Ryman suddenly does a white painting, everyone cheers and ticks white off the list then looks for the next thing, but rather the shared fascination in observing someone going through the intellectual processes that lead to this or that physical embodiment of it—lectures, texts, paintings—to produce artefacts that map ways of thinking. Surely this is what art can offer, at the very least.

CK: Yes … but not in the least. It's the opposite: in the best case. That's what I meant to imply.

SB: So with regard to art in 2007 you mean there's so much between you and the wall, so much to get through before you *can* get to the work … to such an extreme that work is in danger of short-circuiting itself, of stalling the audience in its slowness? To reframe the question slightly, why are certain novels—surely the slowest of mediums—so comparatively compulsive, so engaging, in a way that exhibition art so rarely is?

CK: I read maybe a hundred books a year, so two a week, but almost always pocket books, crime stories, definitely not high literature. Once you're

Stählemühle
MÜNCHHÖF

Doppel=Korn

—— 38 % Vol. ——

∗ JONATHAN MEESE'S ∗

Original
GETREIDE-DADDY

· ERNTESCHACH DEM DÄMON ·

Bäuerliches Erzeugnis · 0,7l

HEGAU-BRENNEREI STÄHLEMÜHLE, 78253 EIGELTINGEN-MÜNCHHÖF
C. SCHOELLER & C. KELLER, WWW.STAEHLEMUEHLE.DE

C K☙ 07.1   J ✳2005✳   Flasche Nr.

Meese

J. MEESE   MAI 2007

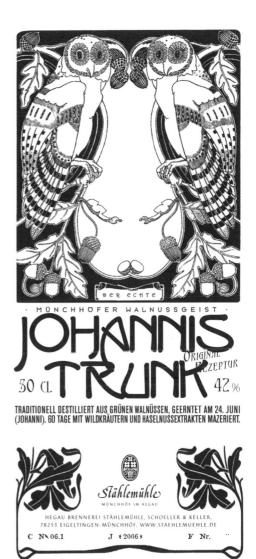

DER ECHTE

· MÜNCHHÖFER WALNUSSGEIST ·

JOHANNIS
TRUNK
ORIGINAL REZEPTUR
50 CL   42 %

TRADITIONELL DESTILLIERT AUS GRÜNEN WALNÜSSEN, GEERNTET AM 24. JUNI
(JOHANNI). 60 TAGE MIT WILDKRÄUTERN UND HASELNUSSEXTRAKTEN MAZERIERT.

Stählemühle
MÜNCHHÖF·IM HEGAU

HEGAU BRENNEREI STÄHLEMÜHLE, SCHOELLER & KELLER,
78253 EIGELTINGEN-MÜNCHHÖF, WWW.STAEHLEMUEHLE.DE

C N☙ 06.1   J ✳2006✳   F Nr.   ¨

43%
70 cl

Stählemühle
MÜNCHHÖF

Schwarzer Abt

Münchhöfer Schwarzriesling

TRAUBENBRAND

2 0 0 6

Im Eichenfaß gereift

HEGAU-BRENNEREI STÄHLEMÜHLE, 78253 EIGELTINGEN-MÜNCHHÖF
SCHOELLER UND KELLER, WWW.STAEHLEMUEHLE.DE

C SA⚹06.1   J ⚹2006⚹   F Nr.   ¨

Stählemühle
MÜNCHHÖF

Waldhimbeer Geist

42%

Edel-Obergeist · 0,5 l · Deutsches Erzeugnis

HEGAU-BRENNEREI STÄHLEMÜHLE, 78253 EIGELTINGEN-MÜNCHHÖF
SCHOELLER & KELLER, WWW.STAEHLEMUEHLE.DE

C WH⚹06.1   J ⚹2006⚹   F Nr.

Die Waldhimbeeren für diesen Geist stammen aus den rauhen Wäldern der Karpaten und garantieren ein stark aromabetontes Geschmacks-erlebnis. Wie bei einem guten Geist üblich, sind die massiven Fruchtnoten besonders intensiv ausgeprägt – und wie es sich für Wildfrüchte gehört: bei diesem Spitzendestillat schmeckt man nicht nur die Süße der Beere, sondern auch die herben Töne von Nadelbäumen und Wildkräutern mit.

through with a few hundred, you're done, so you have to dig harder for new names and even more inferior stuff—but for me it doesn't matter, I'm still completely into the new inferior book in exactly the same way as the good ones.

I would never do this with an art show. If I was in New York, say, and I'd read that gallery such-and-such had an exhibition of so-and-so, I'd never go … only if I already knew the gallery or the artist, that they're doing good things, whatever that means. But where does that knowledge come from? It's the same as the aura I mentioned with Revolver: in the end it's all about biographies. As odd as it might sound, in 2007 biography is art's primary form, in the same way that a specific style of narrative is to the crime story.

SB: Howard Singerman sums this up very succinctly in his book *Art Subjects*. He compares two art magazines, one from the 1940s and one from now, where the text on the cover has changed from being a list of subjects or techniques, to a list of names …

CK: Yes, that's exactly what's happening, but again, *why* is it happening? Personally, I think it's precisely because art has become so complicated. It's so thoughtful—that's the irony—because artists aren't just dealing with formal solutions, with overarching general projects, but with specific research and definite subject matter …

SC: Has contemporary art become too thoughtful, or too specific?

CK: I wouldn't qualify it like that, I just think it's ironic. I like art myself which is para-scientific, which contains information I might be interested in anyway, but is examined in interesting ways, with different parameters and techniques to those usually used by scientists, journalists, or whoever; work which has been researched in new ways. At the same time, I can see that this is problematic, because it requires a lot of texts and therefore publications in advance of any exhibition—or, better, a curator standing next to you explaining what you're seeing, otherwise you can't work it out or make the connections. I always find myself using the example of that piece by … shit, I wanted to say Oscar Wilde! … [*long pause*]

SB: Henry Moore?

CK: No! [*laughs*] … the dandy … [*claps*] … Cerith Wyn Evans! … and specifically, his vertical ray of light in Venice. It's a perfect example of something you can never understand unless someone tells you everything about it, then it's completely interesting. If you simply stand in Venice and see a vertical light beam, you'd just think it's just from some shitty provincial disco. Anyway, as a backlash to that kind of thing the only thing that's really interesting otherwise are the names. I don't mean to be cynical here, even though I know it sounds that way—but the main interest now is how someone got in this magazine, why certain careers are successful, what did they have to do to get there, and so on.

SB: As an art in itself, you mean? The social aesthetics … the mechanics …

CK: Yes, and you see this total change very transparently at the art schools, where I generally go to tell or teach something about books and their relation to art. Increasingly, the students already know exactly what they want, how to use them, the networks, what kind of aspect of their work has to be reproduced, what kind of context it has to appear in.

SB: Again, Singerman captures this very well, describing how in contemporary art schools students aren't taught how to make art, as such, but how to *be contemporary artists*. This is an important distinction because totally based on an existing, exterior model, rather than forging a new, interior one. Ultimately that has to have a limiting or homogenising effect.

A bottle of clear Williams Pear
schnaps is opened and poured

SC: How did you end up out here living and distilling schnaps on a farm in the middle of rural Bavaria after living in Frankfurt? Earlier, you mentioned being fed up with the art world —were you actively or symbolically dropping out of it by moving here?

CK: Well, one of the main reasons for giving up the publishing was through being increasingly involved with all the subventioned publications I mentioned. Making books with so many vested interests and the control that the commissioning institutions assert—at whatever level up the food chain—simply tends to result in books that people don't really want or need; books without reason, or perhaps *soul* is a better word.

So the publishing wasn't very fulfilling, intellectually, and at the same time we were typically dreaming of moving to the countryside like everyone else. We loved the idea of slowing down life, especially with regard to the children, to give them an alternative to metropolitan living, with animals and food you could see growing —if they wanted, not dogmatically. Then we found this farm in a newspaper ad which, among the usual details, contained this phrase 'Right to burn'. We had no idea what that meant—it might as easily have meant the house was only good for firewood!—then we discovered it referred to the distilling rights which came along with the property. In German 'distilling' comes from *Brennen*, which means 'to burn', because you're essentially burning produce.

So we came here, saw the distillery, and the former tenants explained that it was only used to distill wheat, which is what most of the farmers round here usually do. That's how you make the most alcohol—it doesn't cost much to produce and pays the most money. A hundred kilos of wheat costs five Euros at the most. We were just talking about subvention in European art, but that's nothing compared to subvention in European farming, which is virtually total and so extreme that it's getting to the point where, of course, farmers don't *care* what they harvest any more. It's not important to them because they only get money for the *surface* of what they're cultivating.

SC: So it's purely quantity over quality ...

CK: Yes, and also at the moment they get money for grain if they bring it to the bio-gas facilities where they burn it for energy. Farmers get more money for burning it as fuel than for bringing it to a mill to produce flour. Anyway, we discovered that you *have* to distill at least every third year or you lose the right to do it, so we decided to go ahead and learn. I read a lot about it, which I wasn't anticipating, but it quickly became very interesting. Perhaps that's the law of dilettantism: as soon as you start getting interested in

something by reading or researching, it automatically gets *more* interesting, a self-generating energy.

Obviously there are a lot of connections between producing alcohol and art because its the same form of experimentation, it's a research-based activity, it involves knowing a lot, doing a lot, and acquiring experience because you can always improve. It's also very time-consuming ... but in the end it's fundamentally a beautiful alchemistic process which turns this pile of rotten fruit into this pure white—no, transparent—liquid that smells and tastes fantastic. My fascination with distilling is that it's such an old technique— 4000 years old, maybe even 10,000. If you think about the fact that a bunch of people had this idea to heat something up and separate the different evaporation points simply to see what they get from it ... such a simple technique and in the end it produces this form of magic.

SB: And it's more satisfying working with a bunch of apricots than, say, Jonathan Meese?

Prolonged laughter

CK: Yes. Well, no, actually ... it was also great to work with Jonathan Meese, I have to say. Funnily enough we actually just made a Jonathan Meese wheat schnaps for a bar he's making in the house where Marx was born. But, yes, it is a lot more satisfying and interesting working with fruit farmers than all the various parties usually involved in subventioned publishing, that's for sure.

SB: This implies that some or all of the dissatisfaction of working in publishing we've been talking are solved—or resolved—by working in alcohol. Is this because the distribution of labour hasn't changed in the same way? Perhaps the print industry could be described as having changed from 'The Black Art' to 'The Transparent Art' ... which is odd as you just referred to alcohol's transparency in the opposite sense, as a positive thing.

I mean 'transparent', of course, with regard to the effects of desktop publishing, namely the availability and affordability of hardware and software, the so-called democratisation of what was once a professional trade to a point where it doesn't really exist anymore, or at best in a fractured, barely recognisable form, and the related sense that anyone can do it and everyone can see how it's done; the outcomes being the familiar tropes of our condition—lack of specialisation, blurring of roles, transient labour, et cetera. All of which follows the logic of advanced capitalism, but with a resultant chaos and anxiety which is proving a very difficult place to work from, a very unstable place, especially if you can still recall an earlier era where roles were more comfortably demarcated.

Anyway, my question [*laughs*] is: do you have a sense of reclaiming something that was missing by the end of Revolver by experiencing an industry still as controlled and traditional as alcohol production in the manner you practice it here, where the labour processes and roles remain distinct, perhaps emphasized by the small scale, the isolation, the interest in the alchemy … it all seems much more … human-sized.

CK: Absolutely, but also, as a book designer and editor you're not the author—you're more or less a service, and therefore only more or less involved. In producing agriculture, though, you *are* the author … although kind of from God's grace … if you know what I mean.

SC: The apricot is stronger than you!

CK: Kind of, yeah. I don't think of these things in terms of a big unchanging omnipresent creation, because these things *can* actually be modified, but still, I'm essentially working with material I haven't invented—that's the difference … and I have to find the people who make those things with the same love, because for sure 99% of the quality of this schnaps is the fruit, and only 1% is the art of the distiller. From good fruit you get good schnaps, from bad fruit you never do, it's that simple.

It might appear an isolated process, working out here on the farm, but it's not at all … it involves a community and a network, and this is why I include these small texts on the bottles in addition to the obvious name labels, which go into some detail about the varieties of the spirits, and often include which farmer I got the fruit from, just to point out that you need these specific people to make this specific drink, and all are equally essential. But I like that idea of 'The Transparent Art' so much because of the idea I keep mentioning about the objectivity —or the subjectivity!—and that's the point!— in the end it doesn't matter, both are the same with schnaps.

CK: There's one other thing I can try and relate very quickly, and that's something to do with coming from a city to the country with no prior relation whatsoever to farming, which is best described as a fascination for the utterly out-of-balance economy of nature, which is unlike anything experienced in a metropolis. Take the salad we were just eating, for example. If I calculate my hours in the sense of what we think of as a regular fee for labour, or even minimum wage, it would cost something like $30, accounting for the time I spend in the greenhouse, seeding, caretaking, and so on, and the same with the animals—so it's com*pletely* out of balance with any way of economic thinking we've grown up with elsewhere.

On the other hand it's such a great feeling to actually *do* this work, even when it's bad, if it's raining or I'm tired, or things are going wrong … and in the end I work a hell of a lot for a tiny little bit of food. Again, on paper, it's financially crazy because you could go to the best top-quality organic supermarket and buy this salad for much less …

A glass is knocked over and shatters

CK: Ah … sorry … but of course there's some other quality which is less easy to define or relate —a feeling, a sense of rightness and equilibrium. It's very simple: I donate a certain part of my day to work for my food.

SB: It reminds me of something else. Remember when Jan Verwoert was here, talking about communities, and he began with this very simple idea that we're a self-made community borne out of mutual sympathies—and this can apply equally to the magazine or Revolver, as it can to the farm, or any of its various microcosms of animals, plants, fruit, or schnaps. These are groups and relations formed *for their own sake*, not towards any explicit end or result except their own continued existence—and here I mean rather than existing towards an explicit capital-P Political or other capital-S Social end. This struck me as one of those notions which is so stupidly obvious that you can't see it until it's suddenly refracted through someone else's words.

I had a similar experience recently working in the basement bookstore. I suddenly felt like I realised for the first time what capitalism was —by which I mean not as an abstract system I'm vaguely conscious of being complicit in at some indeterminate remove, but in the light of a customer standing in front of me holding a book and asking how much it costs—at which point my reflex is to answer, *whatever you're willing to pay for it*. It was quite a shock to be reminded in this way how value is arbitrary, to *feel* it rather than have it *described* by a philosopher or politician or journalist. I guess this is the same hands-on practicality you're talking about with the farm—primitive in its obviousness but still embarrassingly revelatory [*laughs*].

I'm not sure whether this is leading to a question—maybe only to another drink—but there seems to be some relation between all this: the community whose point of connection is simply a way of thinking, or a sympathy for the others' ways of thinking, and the allocation of time spent preparing your own food, that describes a kind of circular, self-feeding energy. Again, not *towards* something else—not to sell, to decide, prove, or invent something, particularly—but to *exist*, to maintain, to continue, to sustain. It's a circular rather than linear way of thinking. Money is essentially just removed from the equation, and the new equilibrium is a balance of other elements instead.

CK: It's also crucially based in the present rather than the future or on some idea of an end result, an attitude concerned with the here and now, with effort and commitment. It comes back to the various art systems we're involved in, which — particularly at the moment—revolve around this idea of *only doing things because ...*—because someone else invites you to, or will pay you to, or because you'll gain some perceived outcome ... money, respect, fame, further invitations, whatever. The idea of getting together or making something without those preconditions is becoming increasingly rare, and that's a shift for the worse.

For me the reasons for spending time growing these things is also just a simple reaction to not being able to find value or satisfaction in other things. Today I can say I've never felt more satisfaction than when I spend an afternoon here in the stables, for example. Why should I spend so much time doing things like publishing when I could also spend it generating food and drink for myself and family and friends? That feeling only increases, then becomes an obsession, because if you have a farm suddenly you're bound to think about the idea of 'land' which, of course, you don't have to consider in the city. As an artist anyway, you're now trained to live as flexibly as possible—*don't own anything, have your suitcase packed and ready*—but if you're on a farm one of the things you find you're suddenly responsible for is the ground, very literally, with a heritage to consider. If we didn't mow the meadows correctly the farmers next door would come and say, *hey, this isn't good enough*—there's an inherent ethos that the land has to be cultivated properly.

Again, it's simple and obvious, you own something and suddenly it's important to maintain it. Owning becomes interesting again. Take livestock, for instance, which involves the responsibility for their lives, a completely different relationship to the possessions we're used to. Spending time with the animals becomes a complex thing, because it's not solely—or visibly, or immediately—about money. It doesn't work in the same way.

SB: And the new value is a certain intensity of feeling?

CK: It sound very kitsch but it's very true.

SB: 'Intensity of feeling' is quite clear in terms of the publishing and distilling, but less obvious in terms of ownership. It's interesting to consider the idea of 'owning things' as being fundamental to both capitalism and your farming existence, even though we're generally implying they're opposites. Perhaps it's the difference between the hollowness of *gratification* and richness of *responsibility*; you're distilling the good parts of the idea of ownership. That's pushing it a bit, but you understand what I mean.

CK: Yes, again it's to do with taking care of things. I've never really spoken about this with anyone before, but sometimes I need two hours in the evening to just walk around and look at everything ... and though I've seen it many times, it's nothing to do with pride, it's simply about watching ...

Stählemühle
MÜNCHHÖF

Waldhimbeer
· LIKÖR ·

Die Himbeeren für diesen
fruchtigen Likör stammen aus
den ausgedehnten Waldlandschaften
der Slovakei. Wild gesammelt,
handverlesen und sorgfältig
gereinigt werden sie in ganz
leicht angegorenem Zustand
mit unserem Himbeergeist
60 Tage mazeriert und mit
Kandiszucker und Wildkräutern
zu unserer fruchtig-frischen
Likörspezialität verarbeitet, die
zu jedem Anlass – als Apéritif
oder Digéstif passt.

50 cl · 28% vol.

Deutsches Erzeugnis

HEGAU-BRENNEREI STÄHLEMÜHLE, 78253 EIGELTINGEN-MÜNCHHÖF
SCHOELLER & KELLER, WWW.STAEHLEMUEHLE.DE

C HL⸗ 06.1   J ⸎2006⸎   F Nr.   ‥

STÄHLEMÜHLE ARTEMISIA IST EIN ERFRISCHEND HERBER KRÄUTERLIKÖR AUF WERMUT-
BASIS. DER FRUCHTIGE GESCHMACK DES NATURTRÜBEN GOLDBITTERS ENTFALTET SICH
AM BESTEN IM LIKÖRGLAS AUF ZWEI EISWÜRFELN MIT EINER HALBEN SCHEIBE ZITRONE.

Die Kirschpflaume oder auch Myrobalane (prunus cerasifera) gehört in Zentraleuropa leider mittlerweile zu den vernachlässigten, vom Aussterben bedrohten Pflaumensorten. Der volkstümliche Name „Türkenkirsche" (in pfälzischer Mundart auch „Därgelkirsche") weist auf ihre Abstammung aus Mittel- und Kleinasien hin. Im Mittelalter wurden einzelne Pflanzen aus Persien nach Europa gebracht, wo sie heute nur noch vereinzelt an Waldrändern, Bachläufen und aufgelassenen Obstplantagen zu finden ist. Aus brenntechnischer Sicht ist das Verschwinden dieser exotischen Pflaumenart äußerst bedauerlich, ergibt doch die kleine, dunkelrote und säuerliche Frucht ein außergewöhnlich interessantes und intensives Destillat. Das exklusive Aroma unseres Türkenkirschbrandes, den wir ausschließlich von eigenen, handgepflückten, handverlesenen und per Hand (!) eingemaischten Früchten gewinnen, besticht durch seine individualistische Wildheit und ein ungewöhnliches Temperament zwischen Pflaume, Schlehe, Zibarte und Sauerkirsche! Eine absolute Rarität für Liebhaber von Edelobstbränden der Spitzenklasse.

HEGAU-BRENNEREI STÄHLEMÜHLE, 78253 EIGELTINGEN-MÜNCHHÖF
SCHOELLER & KELLER, WWW.STAEHLEMUEHLE.DE

C TK‹ 06.1   J ‹ 2006 ›   F Nr.

looking properly … *what happens over here, what happens over there … those plants are dying now, those plants are growing … the tiles have come off the roof here …* just checking the status of things. It's almost embarrassing to describe this walk, but that's what happens; it's a strange level.

SB: It's getting late. Maybe we should talk about labels on the bottles, seeing as we're pretending that's the reason for the whole conversation.

CK: Okay, but let's taste the most uncreative one first. This is the basic wheat schnaps made from pure grain.

A bottle of Doppel-Korn wheat schnaps is opened and poured

CK: This is only wheat and yeast, so it tastes like bread. That's what people drink in huge amounts in the north of Germany, if it's cheaply done—this is the one for getting drunk, to slowly kill yourself, basically. If distilled well, with care, however, it can also be very tasty. So … the labels. Our basic idea is to create a product which is nurtured and nutritional, made slowly, with craft, how most people imagine the ideal of food and drink, as organic, homemade, hand-cooked, and so on. In this case those ideas are very extreme because every single stage involves this kind of attention.

We harvest the fruit, then crush it, and often we mash it by hand rather than at a mill because we believe this process retains more of the aroma. Also, if a lot of the cores break they release a poisonous blue acid, so I stand there for, say, five hours at a time, squashing the fruit in my hand. This is where all the knowledge of enzymes, chemistry, acids and different kinds of yeasts comes in. Because scientists isolate and introduce new enzymes all the time, there are always new kinds of movements going on, splitting the fruit in different ways which yield different aromas. Basically, the mash should be as liquid as possible. The aroma molecules attach to the alcohol elements, so the more liquid they are the easier they can get together.

SB: Like any Friday night in any community …

CK: We then want to make it clear that this is how we're distilling: traditionally, slowly, with this much care and attention, which is where the labels come in. They're deliberately conservative. All the people from the clubs and the official-professional side of schnaps absolutely *hate* my labels.

SB: But they're 'conservative' in quotation marks, right? Self-consciously conservative, I mean.

CK: Well, more neo- or post-conservative, I would say. Does something like 'post-conservative' even exist!? [*laughs*] On a 'good' schnaps label according to the schnaps people, there has to be a photograph of a fully ripe fruit and golden lettering.

SB: Which is surely conservative *without* quotation marks. Isn't yours is a style, a signifier, rather than *being* conservative …

CK: Not exactly, no. I would say that those guys with the ripe photos are betraying our tradition in the sense that, in my opinion of what schnaps is and means, the heritage, they really *should* look like this—like ours—in some way.

SB: Ah, you mean in the same way as the tradition of the baseball outfits, whereas the ripe fruit labels are more like soccer kits?

CK: Ha! Exactly, yes! A good soccer kit should just have those socks with a couple of stripes, single colour shorts, and a plain matching top. Conservative—like I said! With some of the varieties, though, the labels also refer to a specific historical period. The high time for corn schnaps was after the First World War until a little bit after the Second World War, for example, so we used these particular period vignettes; then the Green Widow Absinthe has this strange Art Nouveau label for obvious reasons.

Sometimes we even make these references through the language … for example the term *Deutsches Erzeugnis*, meaning 'German product', which has it's own strange history. Before the mid-nineties it was mandatory to include that on the bottle, but now the connotations are more Nazi than anything else, and is also completely crazy considering the EU, especially since these are all very obviously local products and everybody knows we only really sell them in this area. So we play with that, or similarly 'Agricultural product' because if you're a *bona fide* distiller you have to include that to distinguish from industrially-produced schnaps. Of course the joke now is that the industrial distillers try and make their products look as agricultural as possible—with a little farmhouse on the label, and so on. So we use particular text, particular typefaces and so on. The only other condition for the labels is that they also have to be fit to be printed out on my laser printer! [*laughs*]

SB: So you're really back to the first days of Revolver …

SC: And the bottles are sold locally?

CK: Well, I'm not legally allowed to export them because all us distillers have some kind of tax reduction. It's not actually that true, but that's how it's described.

SB: And what are the percentages of distribution like, including the government?

CK: In the case of, for example, the wheat schnaps, 60% goes directly to the government.

SC: 60%!?

CK: Yes, that's the tax. The whole system is completely feudalistic: the rules are based on something written in 1830, then written again in 1937, I think … and it's still the law. A feudal system basically means you're allowed to distill, but the state has the monopoly, and you're tolerated as long as you supply most of it as a proportional tax: *we let you make so many litres a year as long as you give us so many litres a year.*

SC: And what do they do with it?

CK: They sell it to pharmaceutical companies, who refine it, neutralise it, and use it for medicine. Obviously you don't do this with expensive fruit schnaps—you pay tax with the wheat and apple schnaps, or in equivalent money, which is also possible. I can't export internationally, but I can sell it in Germany. Otherwise, at the moment, apart from local restaurants, most of the sales are actually from the art crowd buying it through word-of-mouth. If they buy one, they buy six more, and so on. We've just made a deal with one bigger place who'll buy 200 bottles at a time,

then we've done a few artists editions. Before we finish with the absinthe we should make a short detour and try this *likör*, which is traditionally the ladies' drink, made from herbs, and which doesn't contain much alcohol; something like Ramazotti or Averna.

A bottle of Artemisia Goldbitter, a herbal likör, is opened and poured

SB: You did an interview a while back with Maria Fusco about teaching, in which all your responses were lines from your cheap crime stories …

CK: Yes, she re-used a questionnaire by Paul Thek from the 1970s or 80s. They were questions which he put to himself, I think …

SB: Right, and as far as I recall, your replies, or maybe the footnotes to the replies, related your belief that teaching should be founded on teaching specific craft skills rather than personal development, or let's say what have become the more psychiatric tendencies of contemporary art teaching.

CK: Yes, though I would call them 'methods' rather than 'skills'.

SB: But was this a straight response? I remember I'd forgotten your answers were actually quotations, and then couldn't work out whether they genuinely reflected your own views.

CK: The actual answers to the main questions —the detective quotes you mention—didn't mean anything. I mean, if you're Paul Thek—the most esoteric idiot you could imagine—they could mean something because they could mean anything. The only serious response in terms of what I actually believe in are in the footnotes, which are about the 'methods' you're talking about.

SB: I'm trying to formulate a related question in light of all we've talked about, but I'm not sure what it is. Can you make one yourself? [*laughs*]

CK: Well, those answers were tied to a very specific experience. Through a few strange events I became a professor at an art school in Hamburg, which as you know is a big deal in Germany because it's well paid, you're working for the state, they can't fire you, and so on, a bit like tenure in the U.S. Anyway, that school is very much based on ideas of the 1970s, so everything is 'anti-authoritarian'—in quotation marks again—all about 'building personalities'. The students they take on are very young … 18, 19 … usually directly from school, and naturally they have no idea what they want to do, no idea what they want from you, from life, and your job is to 'build these personalities' … it drove me crazy.

SB: That's the school's explicit mandate?

CK: Well, first you get a lot of literature, as a teacher, then you meet the others who have been there for 30 years, with the beards and all that, and then they tell you, this is what we do and how to do it. So of course the first thing is to say well, I don't believe in that so I'll do something different, but after only one year I was so frustrated because nothing was moving. I remember one girl, typical of this situation, who was in a band. The whole time she was there all she did was make posters for her band … which was completely fine, just not art, in any sense whatsoever.

My response, however, was immediately ignored in light of the overriding idea that this was part of her personality! So what!? I couldn't see why I was supposed to be teaching them —I don't know—ethics, morals, character. There was no objective criteria whatsoever, and of course they had no time for grading or evaluating. This is what I meant about the Paul Thek questions—they're *only* about belief, which I just don't see as relevant to art. I quit after a year, and that's what the interview response was based on. How's the herb thing?

Silence

SC: It's a little too much like medicine …

CK: Ah, too bitter! … let's counteract it with a really sweet one, then.

A rogue bottle of Raspberry Likör is opened and poured

CK: This one's not actually made by me but by a neighbour, Frau Braun. [*sips, considers*] Yes, it's very … sugary. She makes some kind of syrup with raspberry juice and mixes it with neutral alcohol, unlike ours which is based on the ghost. This gets slightly complicated to explain, but basically we put the *spirit* of the fruit into it. There are two different ways to make schnaps. One is to distill the actual fruit, and the alcohol is produced from the sugar in the mash which carries the aroma with it—this is what is called fermenting. The other is to take neutral alcohol and mix it with the fruit. Instead of fermenting, the neutral alcohol *sucks* the aroma *out* of the fruit. The process used largely depends on the type of fruit, and the latter is better for raspberries. We've always used the first method, however, which involves the 'geist'—a beautiful word, because it means … well, yes, it means 'spirit' … like 'zeitgeist'—the spirit of the times.

SB: What about moonshine?

CK: [*laughs*] What *about* moonshine? It has two meanings, right? One is the product, and one is the act of doing it. So which are you talking about?

SB: The act of doing it … to make the product.

Prolonged laughter

SB: Off the record.

CK: It's actually very dangerous. Another part of this feudal medieval law is that the customs authorities have the right to check on you whenever they want, without notice. In former times they just went around the mountains in October looking for smoke from fires, which usually indicated a distillery. They still check very regularly, though, and when they do they check absolutely everything—the storage, the day's production, whether there's any sugar added to the mash, which isn't allowed, and whether you've produced exactly what you claimed you would. The surplus is what they call moonshine.

SC: Isn't it called that because it's made after hours, by the light of the moon?

CK: Yes, in the swamps in … [*pause*] Mississippi [*laughs*], I don't know. I guess it originally had something to do with prohibition, when you basically *had* to do it to produce anything.

SC: And for those who couldn't afford the official stuff, so would just make it themselves. Basically it's the rough stuff that gets you wasted fast …

CK: Yes, and that's why I asked whether you meant the act or the product, because even if you distill black, cheaply, you can still make a reasonable, clean alcohol, a clean spirit. When distilling you have to make very clear divisions between the pre-run, the heart, and the afterrun. The pre-run is poisonous and the afterrun has all these oils which make it taste bad … but if you want to keep it all, to literally make the most out of it, you simply mix it all together, in which case you also have this very unhealthy thing, which is where all the stories of people going blind come from.

SB: So you're saying it's possible to be moonshining and not actually make moonshine, and also to make moonshine while not actually moonshining?

Hysteria

CK: Actually, I've been fined already for moonshining … because in the end distilling in Germany is, officially, all about money too. One day I was busy distilling 2000 litres of mash, and they came to check up. I'd applied for this quantity, so it was all fine, then they checked the tanks and in the end, after three hours, they said, *well we checked your tanks and found you have 2060 litres in there instead of 2000.* I said it couldn't be—this was mash from Hungary which came with an invoice saying I bought precisely 2000 litres, and they say, *yes, yes, but we measured it and it's 2060.* I was so convinced that I refused to accept it and demanded that they prove it, to which they replied, *well, to prove it we have to open the tanks and basically destroy the whole lot.* So that's that, I'm caught even though I didn't do anything. Then they fined me for the extra 60 litres and the penalty was 22 Euros! … so obviously this was just a symbolic fine, a yellow card. Next time it gets more serious—a red card and I'm off the pitch. It's essentially a system which is out to kill the small industries, like everything else.

SB: Any last thoughts before we start on the absinthe?

CK: Maybe I should just say that, in relation to the surface of what you're interested in here —the change from publishing books to publishing alcohol—I have to confess that my involvement has also changed my idea of what design and designing is, and that's also precisely in terms of thinking about it less as a surface, and more towards to the notion of changing material from one form to another. By the end of Revolver I could maybe understand the *idea* of designing being an act of transformation, of translation, or transposition, but now I understand it more clearly—more transparently—through observing the tangible changes from plants and fruit to other forms.

A bottle of Grüne Witwe, a traditional Absinthe, is opened and poured

as in STYLE: Parnet points out that Deleuze still hasn't responded to her 'treachery', if he thinks that he has a style. Deleuze says he would like to, but asks her what she wants him to say. He says he can answer more modestly by saying that he lives the problem [je le vis]. He says he doesn't write while telling himself that he'll deal with style afterward. After the tape changes, Parnet rephrases the question as: is the composition of a book already a matter of style? And he answers, yes, entirely. The composition of a book cannot occur beforehand, but at the same time as the book is written.

MATHEMATICS AND GREGG

by Graham Meyer

Everyone who's been to first grade knows that 'MOM' upside-down is 'WOW.' There aren't too many pairs like this because the number of reversible letters is so small. Let L_C be the set of capital letters. Let R be the clockwise rotation function, measured in degrees. $R_{180}: L_C \to L_C$. The subset of L_C that is in the domain of R_{180} is {H, I, M, N, O, S, W, X, Z}. R_{180} maps this subset to {H, I, W, N, O, S, M, X, Z}.

Everyone who's been to fourth grade knows that you can make words by turning a calculator upside-down. Specifically, everyone knows that 55378008 spells BOOBLESS, a word that could possibly be used only in this context (but I'm not sure I want to Google it to find out). Let U be the calculator upside-down function and W the set of whole numbers. $U: W \to L_C$. Specifically, $U: \{0, 1, 2, 3, 4, 5, 6, 7, 8, 9\} \to \{O, I, Z, E, H, S, G, L, B, G\}$.

Gregg shorthand is designed for maximum speed, which means that the units that carry meaning require as few movements as possible. Unlike the alphabet, with which disambiguation is important, Gregg worries little about ambiguity and more about simplicity. Simple signs limit the forms, opening the gate to possibilities for play.

Let Gg be the set of Gregg shorthand representations and R_θ as above, where θ is measured in degrees. Now, the shorthand representation of L is a long arc pointing upward. The shorthand representation of B is a long arc pointing right. G, same thing, downward. V, same, left. $R_{90}(L) = B$. $R_{90}(B) = G$. $R_{180}(V) = B$. See the diagram showing mappings of R_θ over Gg.

Reflections are also possible. Translation in the plane is, of course, trivial in terms of meaning—unlike translation between languages, mathematical translation doesn't change shorthand's meaning.

Vowels in Gregg are represented by loops or short curls that connect the consonants to each other. Vowels' size is more important than their orientation. Therefore, we can perform functions on entire words. $R_{180}(base)=save$. $R_{90}(save)=wag$. $R_{180}(hoed)=doing$. $R_{180}(email)=gamy$.

There exist further possibilities if topological equivalence is defined to tolerate some degree of stretching or bending. Going so far as to allow changes of direction, however, threatens to create so few equivalence categories that hidden juxtapositional epiphanies would be papered over. These relationships are beyond the scope of this paper.

What do these unexpected relationships between words in shorthand mean? Not much, intrinsically, but given the linguistic systematicity shorthand is based on, as much as the homophony of *ode* and *owed*. Poems have been built around less.

Manipulating shorthand to mine for correspondences is a game with a pawn in the field of ideas. It is a deeply serious toy, a museum-ready farm tool, a wildflower in a lonely field. A way to play on the thin line between mere communication and esthetic elegance, wordplay and secret poetry.

Q.E.D.

R_0	R_{90}	R_{120}	R_{135}	R_{180}	R_{270}	R_{300}	R_{315}
F	R				P	K	
V	L				B	G	
S	O				S	U	
N			SH	T	N		SH	T
M			CH	D	M		CH	D

as in TENNIS: Parnet asks if Deleuze attended a lot of tennis matches, and he begins to respond, but then returns to the question of Borg as a Christic character, who created mass tennis, and with that, it was a total creation of a new game. With a Borg, one always rediscovers the kind of player who hears the compliments, but feels that he's miles from doing what he wanted to do. Deleuze feels that Borg changed deliberately: when he was certain of his moves, it no longer interested him, so his style evolved tremendously, whereas the drudges stick with the same old thing. Deleuze says that one has to see McEnroe as the anti-Borg.

2)   The old artist and some working today are still
useing an illusion even Mondrian whose ideas were in
a three dimentional conseption, still worked on
canvas. The constructivitus whose ideas were on a
constick basis, they also called for colour in
three dimention yet their work was actually static
and the colour of their material was excepted to a
point. The end product of their research is a
man-made environment. Life does not excist on a
two dimentional basis. When one walks down the
street the sensation is not only a visual one but a
tactful and sound experience. The artist can no
longer concern himself with illusions he must work
on a realistic basis.

The idea of a structure being composed of structural series of
elements which determin the overall shape and function also creating an internal inviroment, is the
construction in all natural phenom-
ena, an ideal example being the cell.
In the cell one has a number of
elements which are working towards a
function and the whole. Similary the
artichectural designer has a set of
elements which limit the design
possibility. He uses a set of elements
the room, corridor, hall, etc., each
element having a function and also
limiting the visual structure of the
whole. The architectural designers
vision is conceived within the
limitation of the materials and the
structural elements.

THE ARTIST AS A PHILOSOPHER

The artist is as the Philosopher.

The artist is not concerned with finding absolutes as is the scientist.

The artist is concerned with finding the boundarys of things and bringing
them back to society.

The artist is concerned with ethics.

The artist is in the position where he can look at the society around him
in a personalised way and make personalised comments.

The artist must question the very nature of society.

The artist must go out and develop his own unique philosophy,develop his
own code and symbolism and constantly question his surroundings.

The artist philosophy should create his image,an observer to gain any
understanding what orientate himself into the artists mode of thought.

I am part of the environmental total.

The environmental total consists of sets and sub sets of variable events.

Sets and sub sets of the variable event are encounted by chance.

The variable event has degrees of randability and probability.

I can not predict an event I can only measure its probability.

The environmental total becomes a random event.

I must learn to live with the random event and except it as an intricate

part of the total whole.

Four early manifestos

STEPHEN WILLATS AND
THE SPECULATIVE DIAGRAM

by Emily Pethick

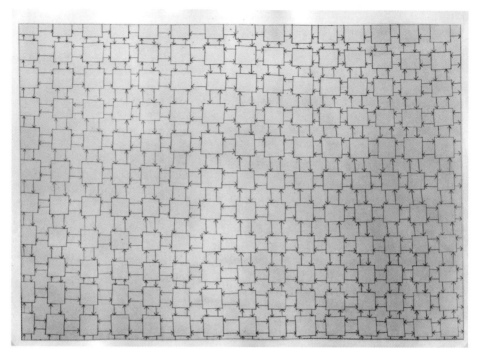

Homeostatic Drawing No. 1 (1968)

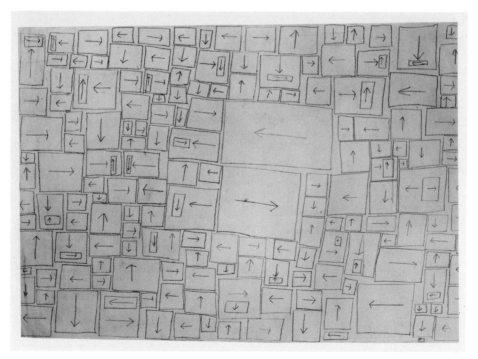

Organic Exercise No. 1, Series 1 (1962)

Since the early 1960s the work of Stephen Willats has focused on social relations and notions of transformation, often through the lens of self-organisation. In the late 1950s Willats began to question a number of contemporary notions concerning the artist, such as the idea of 'genius' and the sense of authority that artists created for their work, which had the effect of sustaining a passive relationship with the audience. He started to draw models of how the artwork may involve the

RESOLUTION LEVEL ONE
PRESENCE

ACTS OF TRANSFORMATION

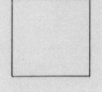

RESOLUTION LEVEL TWO
IDENTITY

RESOLUTION LEVEL THREE
BEHAVIOUR

RESOLUTION LEVEL FOUR
COMPONENTS

RESOLUTION LEVEL FIVE
FABRIC

THE HIGHER THE LEVEL OF
RESOLUTION THE MORE
COMPLEX THE STRUCTURE
VIEWED

Five Acts of Transformation (1998)

participation of the audience, introducing notions of unpredictability into the equation via individual interaction, setting off a more active relationship between artist and the audience, often using the diagram as a way of mapping out these relations.

Whilst studying on the Ground Course at Ealing School of Art, Willats first came across cybernetics, and began to introduce related ideas into his practice as a way of formulating models for social exchange. He went on to work with Gordon

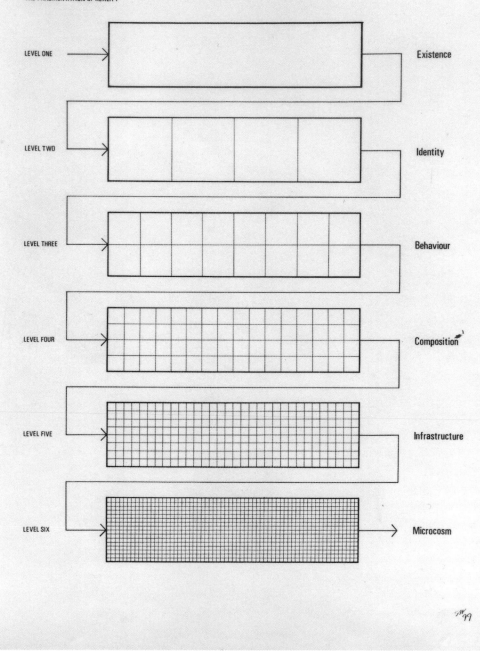

Complex World
SIX LEVELS OF RESOLUTION AND TRANSFORMATION
THE FRAGMENTATION OF REALITY

LEVEL ONE — Existence

LEVEL TWO — Identity

LEVEL THREE — Behaviour

LEVEL FOUR — Composition

LEVEL FIVE — Infrastructure

LEVEL SIX — Microcosm

Complex World (1999)

Pask at System Research, where he also came into contact with black box theory, which states that a system can be fully understood once the inputs and outputs are well-defined without knowledge of the underlying structure, mechanism, and dynamics of the mind, providing a model of working with speculative thought that released people from the complexities of actuality; ideas which influenced Willats' use of the diagram as a way of finding a language around communication processes.

Various *Control* covers

In 1965 he initiated *Control* magazine, which aimed to respond to the current developments in artistic practices, and was centred on the idea of artists explaining practice. The title was derived from the cybernetic idea of 'self-determining models of control' (as opposed to 'hierarchal deterministic models'), thus a model for thinking around ideas of self-organisation. The first issue received contributions from a number of Willats's close friends and colleagues and was printed

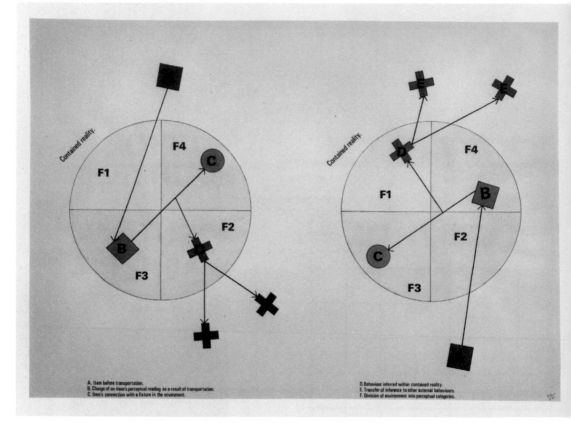

A Model of Perceptual Transformation (1978)

overnight for cash and self-distributed. *Control's* original logo was designed by Dean Bradley who worked for Pushpin Agency in New York and Design Communications in the UK. The screen-printed cover of the pilot number featured a purple dot which was repeated in the centrefold as an edition that could be removed and pinned on the wall above the reader's head as they leafed through the issue [reproduced as a sticker in this issue of DDD]. This dot represented the 'node'

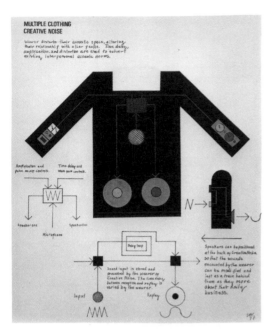

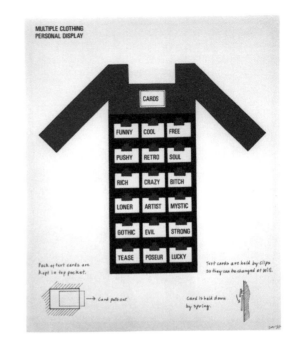

OPEN SYSTEM

The full omni-directional possibilities of language are left open to the wearer in this design. A grid pattern allows any identity, message or feeling to be stated by the arrangement of individual letter panels into horizontal and vertical combinations of words. The assemblage comprises 56 individual white squares with a single bold letter in black, and interconnecting link pieces, with two tops allowing a variety of clothing ideas to be made up. By arranging the letters into the words required, and then using the link elements to attach them into a matrix, complex associations and meanings can be built up between the texts into multi-layered structures. Each square, and link components, have press stud attachments, so that the matrix can be pieced together bit by bit, and remain stable.

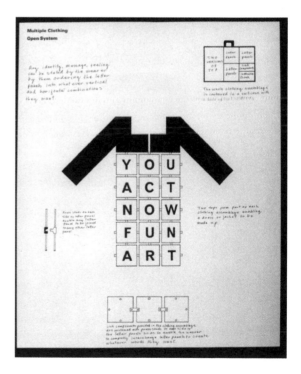

Various examples of Multiple Clothing

—the fundamental unit in any network theory, essential to cybernetics' model of communication, control, and regulatory feedback, and now in common use since the proliferation of digital technology.

Around this same time, in the mid-1960s, Willats had temporarily abandoned his artist-status, describing himself as a 'conceptual designer', and produced 'Multiple Clothing', a series of adaptable designs for clothing that could carry messages, and

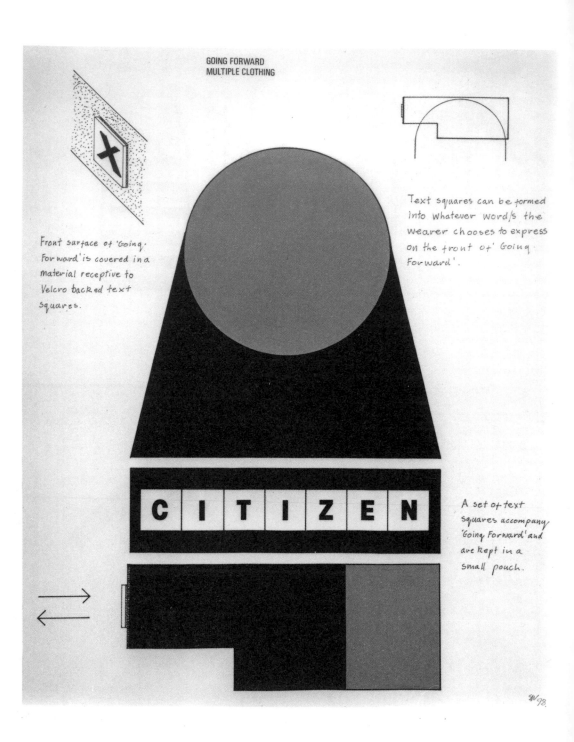

Front surface of 'Going Forward' is covered in a material receptive to Velcro backed text squares.

Text squares can be formed into whatever word/s the wearer chooses to express on the front of 'Going Forward'.

A set of text squares accompany 'Going Forward' and are kept in a small pouch.

Multiple Clothing

flexible modular furniture named Corree Design. Both employed structures that allowed them to be altered, thus emphasising the wearer's imagination and involvement. This idea of personalisation also came into a number of works in which Willats has

worked with communities that inhabit tower blocks. In the 1970s he became interested in the tower block as a polemical ideological symbol within society and in the dynamics between the planning of spaces and the ways in which they are inhabited.

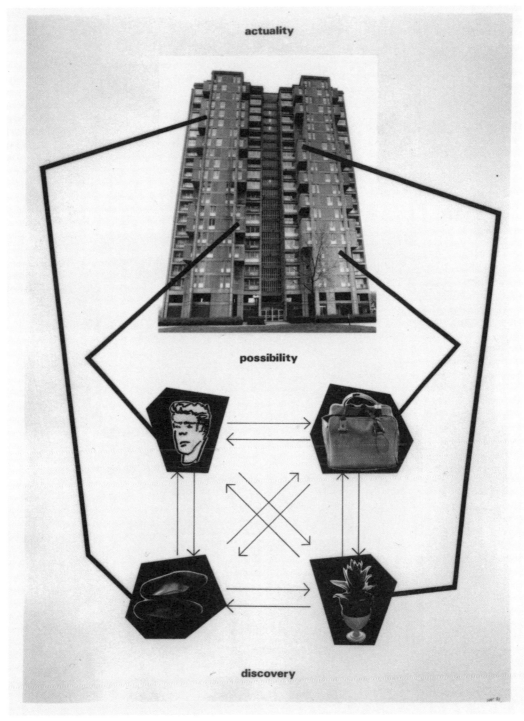

actuality

possibility

discovery

Encounter In The Corridor (1991)

While these buildings were built with progressive social intentions towards the establishment of new communities and ways of living, they were also highly planned environments that influenced and shaped people's lives. As a counter to this, Willats observed the relationships between the rigid structure of these buildings—which represented a form of institutional control—and the reality of life within them, through the ways in which the residents personalised, adapted and shaped their

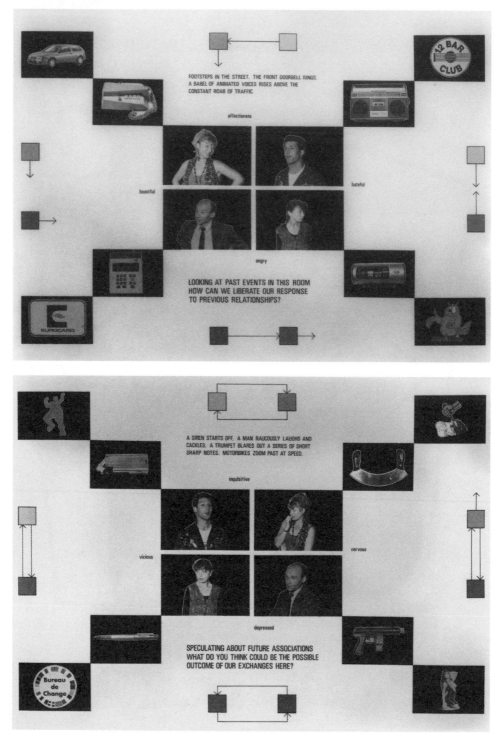

Moving Between The Past Present And Future (1996)

own environments. In creating their own reality, these self-organised spheres originated by individuals become the random elements that changed the structure. This notion of micro- or sub-cultures is also explored more explicitly in the early 1980s in his series of works which recorded the night culture of some of London's secret clubs, where self-organised creativity was flourishing, yet again investigating the edges of culture, outside of the mainstream.

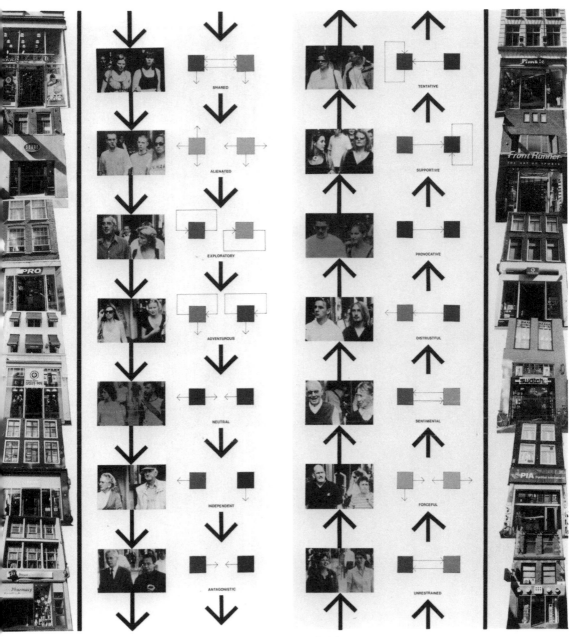

Street Talk, Amsterdam (2004)

Willats has continued to produce work that finds the basis for society in relationships, and the recognition of difference as a starting point for exchange. These create a sense of awareness of oneself in relation to others—be that the artist and audience, or of oneself as part of society. The diagram becomes a tool to create conceptual models for practice, as well as to map more ephemeral and speculative ideas relating to communication and relationships, and the different

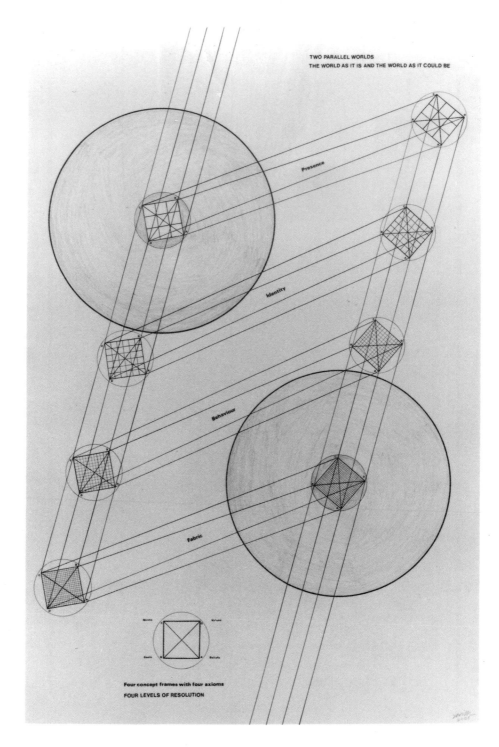

The World As It Is And The World As It Could Be (2006)

levels of complexity within which one can view the
world. It is within these various sets of relations
that are not fixed, but adaptable, that Willats finds
the space for change.

(Image credits are on p. 134)

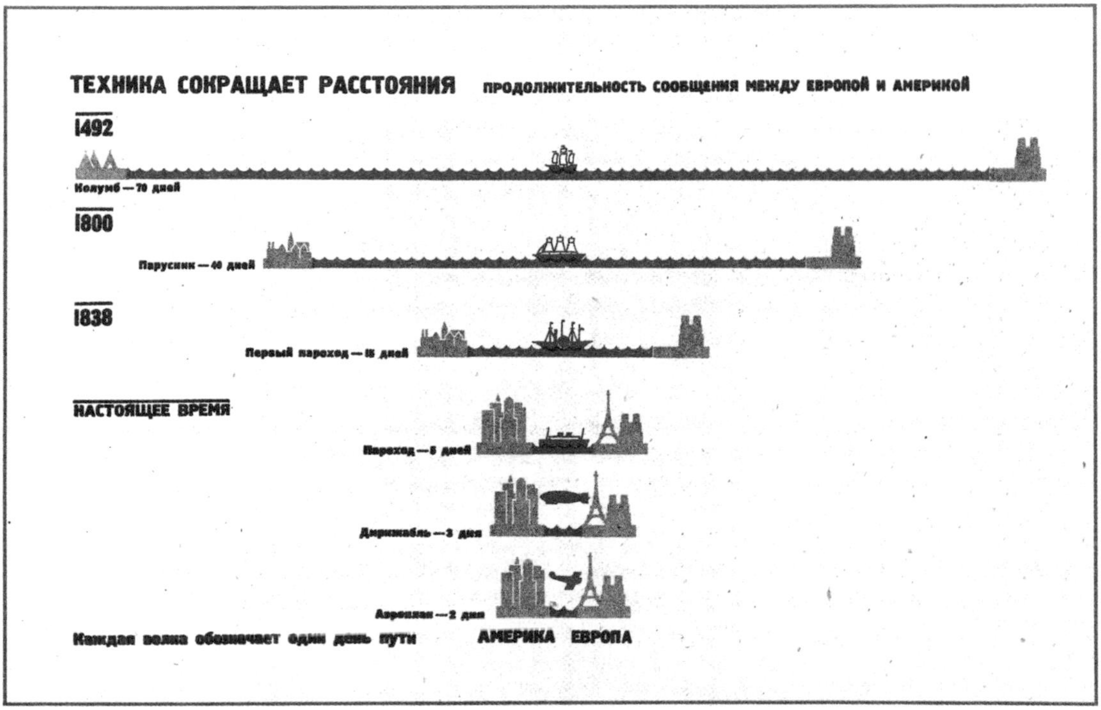

ТЕХНИКА СОКРАЩАЕТ РАССТОЯНИЯ продолжительность сообщения между Европой и Америкой

1492

Колумб — 70 дней

1800

Парусник — 40 дней

1838

Первый пароход — 15 дней

НАСТОЯЩЕЕ ВРЕМЯ

Пароход — 5 дней

Дирижабль — 3 дня

Аэроплан — 2 дня

Каждая волна обозначает один день пути   АМЕРИКА   ЕВРОПА

OTTO NEURATH (1882–1945): A BRIEF BIOGRAPHY

Otto Neurath, the son of a Viennese academic, begins his study into pre-capitalist economies and war economies; from this he develops his ideas on the moneyless economy (or economy in kind)—based on production according to need over the profit motive.

1914–18: Neurath joins the army and his skills as an economist are soon utilised as the planner of supplies for the German army, displaying an organisational skill he would later transfer to many future projects. He is appointed Head of the General War and Army Economics section of the War Ministry in Vienna and at the same time becomes director of the Museum of War Economy in Leipzig. This lays the ground for his later work in Vienna; the aim of the Leipzig museum is to educate on the basis of visual information; to display the whole mechanism of an economy with the use of text, models and statistical tables.

1918–1919: In early November 1918 the German revolution begins with strikes, demonstrations and armed rebellion. After the resignation of Emperor Wilhelm II and King Ludwig of Bavaria, The Bavarian Republic is declared, with the German empire to follow. The war museum in Leipzig is closed down. Having joined the Social Democratic Party, Neurath attempts to push through his plans for a socialised economy.

In January 1919 Neurath travels to Munich to discuss the economy with the president, Kurt Eisner, and to lobby every influential body that will listen to him. In April he is appointed president of the Central Economic Administration and he attempts to institute a programme of socialisation that he believes will take six years to institute. However, the Bavarian Soviet Republic is short-lived and soon falls; Neurath is arrested, tried and imprisoned. He serves a short time of an eighteen-month sentence and returns to a greatly changed Vienna.

1919–34, 'RED VIENNA': In May 1919 the Social Democrats gained control of the Viennese government. Following Max Adler's philosophy of Bildungspolitik (emphasising that education has a vital link to emancipation), a policy of reform affecting everything from housing to education is instituted.

In 1920 Neurath becomes General Secretary of the Research Institute for Social Economy with a remit to support the co-operative housing movement 'in the spirit of social economy'.

In 1921 Neurath also institutes the Co-operative Housing and Allotment

Association, an umbrella organisation for all housing co-ops that plan the construction of houses (with the participation of architects including Adolf Loos and Josef Frank). Neurath wrote: 'The happiness of the inhabitants has to be the measure for housing policy'.

In 1924 Neurath proposes the Museum of Economy and Society, an institution for public education and social information. It is in this context that the 'Viennese Method' (later to be known as ISOTYPE) is developed as a system of visualising statistical data which 'facilitates quick recognition and easy recall'.

In May 1925 the Museum of Economy and Society's first graphical displays are produced. In this year the museum also designs displays for an exhibition on health, social care and sport, which are exhibited in Austria House in Düsseldorf. This is the first display to be seen outside Vienna and causes a sensation. Commissions from foreign countries will soon follow, allowing Neurath to set up bureaus in other countries.

In 1927 the permanent exhibition space of Museum of Economy and Society opens in Vienna's City Hall (the space is designed by Josef Frank). The exhibition deals with the world economy, Germany and Austria, the labour movement and population.

In 1928 Neurath invites Gerd Arntz to join the team. The artist proves to be an invaluable addition. The exhibition 'Mother & Child' opens and the book *Die bunte Weld* [The Colourful World], with drawings by Arntz (1929), is published.

In 1929 touring exhibitions to Berlin, Zagreb, Klagenfurt, Mannheim, The Hague and Chicago are organised. By this time the collection represents a series of graphic elements that are reproducible and inter-changeable. Neurath envisages a series of social museums across the world; the 'mu-seum of the future' is mobile and flex-ible—rather than the people going to the museum, the museum goes to the people.

In 1931 the Soviet embassy in Vienna invites Neurath to establish a Mu-seum of Economy and Society in Moscow. The Council of People's Commissars decree: 'All public and co-operative organisations, unions and schools are directed to use picture statistics according to the method of Dr Neurath.'

In 1933 Chancellor Engelbert Dollfuss suspends the powers of the Austrian parliament and rules by emergency decrees that dissolve the powers of the labour unions and the press.

In February 1934, following two days of armed conflict, Dollfuss assumes total control, abolishing Social Democratic and Communist organisations and purging all public institutions, including the Ernst Mach Society (the vehicle of the Vienna Circle). The Museum of Economy and Society is closed down and its offices searched. Neurath, at this time in Moscow, is warned by Marie Reidemeister not to return to Vienna and he makes his way to The Hague, via Prague.

1934–1940: NEURATH IN THE HAGUE: Joined by Reidmeister and Arntz, The Hague becomes Neurath principle centre of operations from 1934 to 1940. Here he continues his work, establishing the International Foundation for Visual Education in The Hague. Despite the difficult circumstances—the Foundation receiving very few commissions—Neurath managed to organise two conferences (in Paris and Prague) that launch the Unity of Science Movement. The principle members of the Vienna Circle, with whom Neurath has worked with for the past twelve years, have by now been dispersed (Carnap to Prague, Feigl to the USA and Neurath to Holland) or have died (Hahn and Schlick); the conferences provided a way in which the remaining members could meet and increase their international profile.

Other conferences would follow between 1934 and 39. It was in The Hague that Neurath set to work on the encyclopdia project, a modern version of Diderot's great endeavour, establishing an international committee that would oversee its production. (The first monograph was published in 1938).

In 1936 the Unity of Science Institute is established as a part of the Mundaneum Institute in The Hague. In the same year Neurath publishes *International Picture Language* which gives a comprehensive description of the method now known as ISOTYPE. At this time he also publishes *Modern Man in the Making*. Neurath travels to the USA to organise an exhibition on the prevention of tuberculosis. 500 versions of the exhibition are produced and shown throughout the USA.

In 1937 Neurath and his team create a large exhibition 'Rund um Rembrandt' [Around Rembrandt], their last work to be exhibited in the Netherlands during Neurath's lifetime.

1940–1945: As the Germans invade in 1940, Neurath and Reidemeister make their way to Scheveningen harbour and board a lifeboat called the *Seaman's Hope*, the boat is intercepted by a British destroyer and the passengers are taken to Dover. Neurath is interned for eight months. On his release he begins teaching in Oxford and he and Reidemeister set up the Isotype Institute, producing exhibitions, film documentaries (with Paul Rotha) and a series of books. Neurath resumes his work on housing projects and the Isotype Institute produce an exhibition called 'Housing and Happiness'.

On the 22nd of December 1945 Neurath dies suddenly in Oxford. Marie continues to produce work in a series of publications covering a wide range of subjects

Compiled by Steve Rushton.
Source: Nancy Cartwright, Jordi Cat, Lola Fleck & Thomas E. Uebel, *Otto Neurath, Philosophy Between Science and Politics* (Cambridge: Cambridge University Press,1996), pp.7–88. Illustrations by Gerd Arntz.

Kraftwagenbestand der Erde

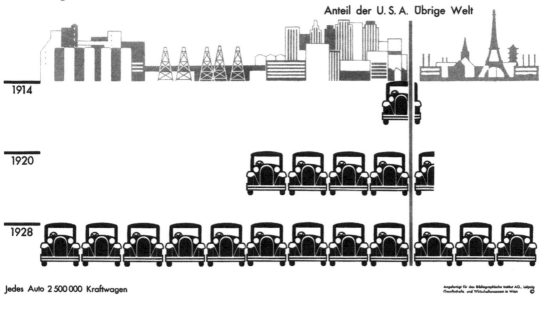

Anteil der U. S. A.   Übrige Welt

1914

1920

1928

Jedes Auto 2 500 000 Kraftwagen

Angefertigt für das Bibliographische Institut AG., Leipzig
Gesellschaft- und Wirtschaftsmuseum in Wien ©

Gesellschaft und Wirtschaft 56

Otto Neurath, *Number of Cars on the Earth*, in the section 'Society and Economy' of *Atlas* (1930), p. 56

Streiks und Aussperrungen

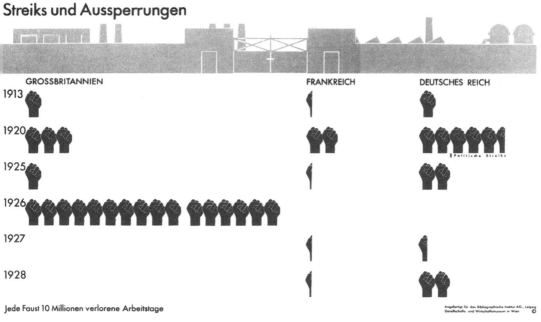

GROSSBRITANNIEN	FRANKREICH	DEUTSCHES REICH
1913		
1920		
1925		
1926		
1927		
1928		

Jede Faust 10 Millionen verlorene Arbeitstage

Angefertigt für das Bibliographische Institut AG., Leipzig
Gesellschaft- und Wirtschaftsmuseum in Wien ©

Gesellschaft und Wirtschaft 88

Otto Neurath, *Strikes and Lockouts*, in the section 'Society and Economy' of *Atlas* (1930), p. 88

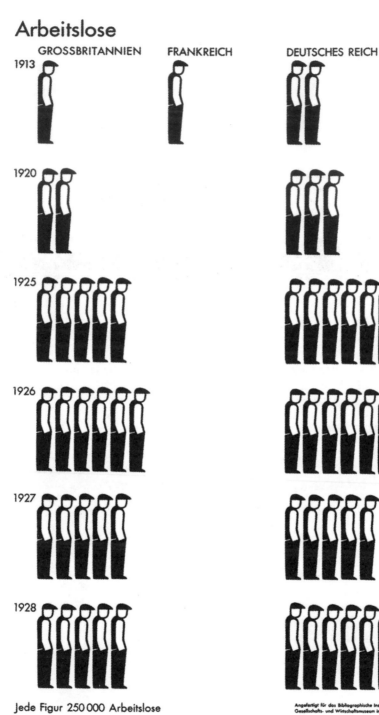

Otto Neurath, *Unemployed*, from the section 'Society and Economy' in *Atlas* (1930), p. 87

LIKE SAILORS ON THE OPEN SEA

by Steve Rushton

1

It is customary to introduce the work of the utopian philosopher Otto Neurath in a manner similar to this:

> Otto Neurath (1882–1945) was a philosopher of science, sociologist, and a political economist. Neurath was one of the leading figures of the Vienna Circle, a logical positivist and a leading light in the Unity of Science movement. Neurath can also be credited with the invention of a system which by the 1930s was called ISOTYPE (International System of TYpographic Picture Education)—a method of representing quantitative information via easily interpretable icons. ISOTYPE was the precursor of the pictogram—the signs that we see every day in airports and on toilet doors.

Now, none of the above is untrue, it's just that it gives a particular emphasis that excludes some very important aspects of ISOTYPE, and it doesn't give us a true indication of the importance and range of Neurath's thought. Firstly, the problem with the story above is that it situates ISOTYPE at an immovable point in history. In this narrative ISOTYPE becomes an interesting historical artifact, a point in a progressive history toward a more efficient system—the pictogram. The story above is useful because people can easily relate to it, because we all have daily experience of the pictogram, and because it's partly thanks to Neurath that we rarely lose our way in airports or walk into the wrong toilet. But such a narritivisation doesn't give due account of the differences between ISOTYPE and the pictogram, nor does it allow for an understanding of the real contemporary relevance of ISOTYPE.

This picture shows Marie Reidemeister working on two sheets of paper at the early stages of the production of an ISOTYPE sheet. On the left-hand page she has written a series of numbers. This is the raw data, the code. On the right-hand page she makes a series of symbols that translate the statistics into pictures. This is the interface. So the relationship between the data and ISOTYPE is similar to the relationship between the code you would see if you cursored to 'view source' on any web page and what you see on the interface of that web page.

Because ISOTYPE converted digital information into pictures, it provided us with a structure of visualisation that encouraged a very contemporary mode of attention; it is through visual technologies such as ISOTYPE that we learned to 'browse'.[1] It is the structural logic of ISOTYPE as a form of filtering software that engenders a particular technology of looking which we take with us every time we surf the web or flick through a magazine. But, of course, something as slippery as a 'mode of attention' isn't as easy to illustrate as a pictogram, even if its implications are more profound.

ISOTYPE from its inception follows the logic of the code that creates it—it is serial, it forms patterns, it creates templates, it is composed of elements that are interchangeable. It was this principle, for instance, that allowed for the production of 500 versions of the exhibition of tuberculosis to be exhibited in every major town in the USA (1936), and also allowed for the possibility to reconfigure different elements taken from a data-base of images that accumulated over time. For us, the logic of ISOTYPE exceeds its technology, and exceeds the historical circumstances that produced it—it enters into us and changes the way we look at things.

2

An encyclopedia and not a system is the genuine model of science as a whole.[2]

Because Neurath's activities are so varied we have difficulty giving him a simple job title—'philosopher' seems to fall short of the mark (and it's a title he didn't encourage), as does 'social engineer', or even 'inventor of ISOTYPE', or by extension 'grandfather of the pictogram'. In truth, Neurath is constantly caught between the categories he sought to unify.

However, Neurath's various activities can be brought together by understanding him as a thinker who was committed to the project of the encyclopedia, an unfinished project that began in the enlightenment—notably Leibniz's *Atlas Universalis*, the work of d'Alembert, Diderot and the French Encyclopedians—all of whom used a combination of texts and pictures in order to display an anti-metaphysical, scientific conception of the world. What interested Neurath about the encyclopedia was that it opposed 'system' in that the knowledge represented within the encyclopedia was always provisional (the encyclopedia always anticipates an updated or revised edition). This is in stark contrast to the idea of knowledge as a system in which we have complete knowledge of present facts from which complete predictions of the future could be made.[3] For Neurath, who understood language as a medium rather than a system, there was no exact place for the mediation of exact science.

The encyclopedia project, therefore, requires a particular conception of how language functions; the debate within the Vienna circle centered around those who understood 'Language as Calculus' (LC) and those, including Neurath, who understood 'Language as a Universal Medium' (LUM). The first (LC) tended to understand language as resembling a system that accorded to universal 'laws' and that the laws of language were as immutable as mathematical equations; this idea is opposed by LUM, which allowed for the difference between the meaning and the use of a particular word or sentence (a famous adherent of this second idea would be Wittgenstein). In adopting the notion of language as a universal medium, Neurath set his face against the conception of science propounded by Descartes and Kant—that scientific laws are universal, that they are true in all ages, and are true irrespective of what any particular person has to say about them—as true as 2+2=4. Neurath, in line with his near contemporary A.N. Whitehead, stressed that the 'laws' of science which we understand to be universal are actually themselves the products of scientific discourse—they are produced within

the practices of science and philosophy and are therefore provisional, as provisional as the language which constructs them. In short, there is no foundation to knowledge—there is no exact place for exact science.

This emphasis was later adopted by Thomas S. Kuhn in his seminal book *The Structure of Scientific Revolutions* and latterly by Bruno Latour in books such as *Laboratory Life* and *Science in Action*. In this scheme scientific 'laws' are produced at the level of practice, through the production of evidence and its subsequent mediation—all of which begs the question: do we discover scientific truth or do we construct it in the manner of a well told fairy tale?

3

We are like sailors who have to rebuild their ship on the open sea, without ever being able to dismantle it in dry dock and reconstruct it from the best components.[4]

This metaphor was re-written by Neurath in a number of different circumstances between 1913 and 1944. In all cases, whether relating to logical empiricism, the visualisation of statistics or the unity of science, it provides us with a metaphor for how we negotiate our understanding of the world. We are born into systems of knowledge, language and economy that collectively serve to define us, but it is also the case that we can be productive agents in shaping the boat in which we float. If, for the provisionalist Neurath, social orders, scientific accounts and the mediative properties of language are all in flux it is nevertheless still possible to give a comprehensive account of the world, in the sense that we can make the world comprehendible by taking existing elements of the boat and reconfiguring them. He did not advocate a totalising theory (or theory of everything) that would be applicable to all ages or which could predict the future, but rather he advocated a more empirical (as in 'given to experience'), even pragmatic, stance with the production of visual and textual technologies that would do justice to the material conditions that shaped our lives, which allowed for a comprehension of those conditions, and also made possible connections that were previously opaque. We see this vision only ever partially realised; in the work done in Neurath's museum project during the First World War, at the Museum of Society and Economy in Vienna in the 1920s and 1930s,

Minenproduzenten in Deutschland

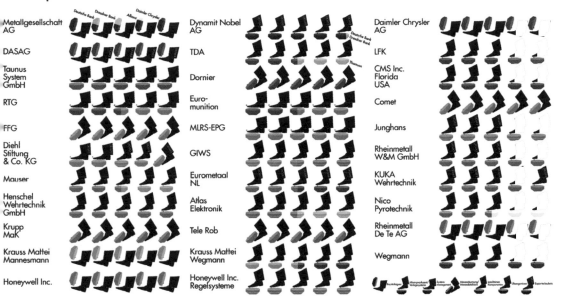

Alice Creischer & Andreas Siekmann, *Landmine Producers in Germany*
Contemporary actualization of p. 28 of *Atlas*, after Neurath/Arntz (in collaboration with
the professors and students of the university of Lüneburg)

Verlegte Landminen, Minenopter, Minenpatente

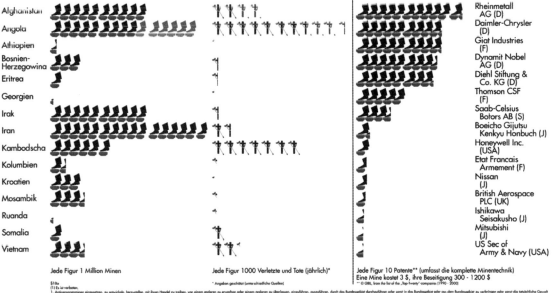

Alice Creischer & Andreas Siekmann, *Planted Landmines, Landmine Victims, Landmine Patents*
Contemporary actualization of p. 25 of *Atlas*, after Neurath/Arntz (in collaboration with
the professors and students of the university of Lüneburg)

or in the various manifestations of Neurath's 'museum of the future', where exhibitions traveled to the people and were reproducible, comprising interchangeable elements which allowed for change and contingency. We also see this vision in publications such as *Atlas* (1930), *International Picture Language* (1936), *Modern Man in the Making* (1939), the unfinished *Encyclopedia of Unified Science*. But if the vision of Neurath was only ever partially realised we can nevertheless clearly see a consistency of method, an epistemology that begins in the enlightenment and carries beyond the modernist project into the present day.

4

The sum-total of human happiness is too small. It should be bigger.[5]

ISOTYPE attempted to make complex information intelligible to the masses in the form of the combination of succinct images and select words. In doing so it sought to reduce complexity through a series of basic units of information that could be commonly understood (even if they are not universally true), it sought to allow for connections between seemingly disparate elements. Neurath the encyclopedian attempted 'to establish contact between disciplines', 'to remedy the plurality of languages', 'to throw bridges between sciences'.[6] Neurath was not alone in seeking out the possibilities of unification and simplification: Ogden's BASIC English, for instance, attempted to reduce the English vocabulary to 800 words (Neurath wrote *International Picture Language* using Basic), and Paul Otlet's Mundaneum attempted to create a repository of the sum of human knowledge along with a system of retrieval and cross referencing. These various projects might stand as monuments to a positivist conception of the world which is no longer viable, or to a utopianism which seems at odds with our current reality. But I would encourage another emphasis when considering these historical objects, an emphasis which gives them a new activity in the present day. They all provide models wherein problems of communication are understood to be software problems, they all provide filtering systems which re-present existing information and allow for new forms of mediation.

If ISOTYPE, Basic English and Otlet's library cataloguing system (which is still used today) can be understood as software they carry with them the pitfalls of software: Software directs the flow of knowledge—what can and cannot be said and what can and can not be asked. For instance, the Frequently Asked Questions on a web site are often the only questions one can ask.

But I would suggest that ISOTYPE invites us to think outside of the existing template, and raises issues which are the current concern of the open source community: what questions should we ask of our world and what technologies should be employed which are appropriate to those questions? These are concerns that ISOTYPE took seriously in order to increase 'the sum-total of human happiness'.

NOTES
1. Fank Hartmann, 'The Quest for an 'Inclusive Form of the Icon', in *After Neurath Symposium*, (The Hague: Stroom, 2006)
2. Neurath cited in Walter Tega, 'Atlas, Cities, Mosaics' in: Nemath and Stadler (eds.), *Encyclopedia and Utopia The Life and Work of Otto Neurath* (Dordrecht: Kluwer Academic Publishers, 1996), p. 65
3. Ibid., p. 65
4. Neurath, 'On Neurath's Boat' in: Cartwright, Cat, Fleck, Uebel (eds.), *Otto Neurath, Philosophy Between Science and Politics* (Cambridge: Cambridge University Press, 1996), p. 48
5. Neurath, *Encyclopaedia and Utopia*
6. Neurath in Tega, p. 64

Steve Rushton recently curated the project *After Neurath*, at Stroom, The Hague, comprising: a symposium, with speakers Frank Hartmann, Robin Kinross, Kristóf Nyíri and Femke Snelting; the exhibition *After Neurath—Like Sailors on the Open Sea* with the artists: Gerd Arntz, Bureau d'études, Alice Creischer & Andreas Siekmann, Stephan Dillemuth, Chad McCail, Oliver Ressler, Thomson & Craighead; and a series of projects by young designers from Koninklijke Academie van Beeldende Kunsten (Type and Media), The Hague and the Jan van Eyck Academy, Maastricht. The project will continue at Stroom with the a project concerning Neurath's relation to architecture, entitled *World Polis*, in late 2007.

as in UN (ONE): Deleuze suggests considering the statement: all bodies fall. What is important, is not that all bodies fall, but rather the fall itself and the singularities of the fall.

SHOOT THE PLAYER PIANO!

by Alex Waterman

This is the story of the player piano and the piano player. It concerns two of the great 20th century pianists, Glenn Gould and David Tudor, their careers as virtuosos and the nature of their relationship to technology and reproduction.

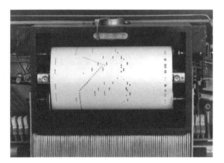

The player piano was invented in the 19th century, an automated version of the piano which plays without a pianist—the keys being struck by mechanical, pneumatic or electrical means instead. Besides being a mass-market product which could equally reproduce high art and popular songs for the wealthy customer in the comfort of their own home, the player piano was also the precursor to punch tape roll, the earliest method of computer programming.

An early analogue computer itself, therefore, the player piano was an odd mongrel of cutting edge technology and staple bourgeois furniture. The subsequent development of the Personal Computer had a similar double origin in the technologies of the typewriter and television, an embodiment and fusing of both 'home' and 'office'. While the player piano offered to 'stand in' for the pianist, however, it did not eliminate the concert hall—the institution that eventually invoked terror and disgust in Gould and Tudor.

While Gould and Tudor represented very different fields of production, aesthetic sensibilities, taste, repertoire, and performance style, both astonished audiences with their idiosyncrasies, eccentricities, and, of course, virtuosity. Technology allowed them to escape from their anxiety-ridden performance careers as concert pianists and settle into more desired roles as, respectively, interpreter and composer. These shifts enabled them to pursue aspects of music production which the concert hall had, for them, eradicated through its bourgeois traditions, expectations and demands.

Thomas Bernhard's *The Loser* (1983) and William Gaddis's *Agapē Agape* (2002) each provide a fictional lens through which to read the life of the virtuoso as a prototype of the artist and his struggle for autonomy in the age of reproduction. *The Loser* is a fictional account of circumstances in which the performer, Glenn Gould, is so technically perfect and ingenious that he obliterates the need for any other. At the same time, unable to bear the false tranquility of the bourgeois contexts in which his work exists, the genius disrupts the flow of life. He catapults onto the stage to radically re-write societal norms, yet is destroyed by the audience's expectations and ends up merely affirming the absurd theatricality of his own rejection of aristocratic and middle class morality. Bernhard's fictional Gould is barely distinguishable from his actual persona. In a 1960s TV interview, for instance, he proclaimed,

> I detest audiences ...
> I think they are a force of evil

Published almost twenty years later, the subject of Gaddis's final novel, *Agapē Agape*, is the player piano rather than the piano player—a mechanical virtuoso rather than a human one. 'Agapē' is an ancient Greek word which 'represents divine, unconditional, self-sacrificing, active, volitional, and thoughtful love'. Like *The Loser*, the book is essentially a reflexive piece of fact-based fiction. Gaddis recounts the history of the player piano to discuss the necessity of failure in art, specifically how mechanical reproduction strips the artist of this most human of possibilities.

Gaddis's thesis is notably similar to that proposed by Walter Benjamin in his cornerstone essay 'Art in the Age of Mechanical Reproduction' (1936), although he was apparently unaware of Benjamin's ideas when he began *Agapē Agape*. Ultimately, the book is a self-conscious example of its thesis: the key narrative conceit is the author's inability to write a book of the same name. Close to death himself, the curious story Gaddis ends up recounting is that of a dying writer trying to articulate the intellectual property of his life's work at the same time as dividing his physical property in the form of a will. In Bernhard's work Gaddis found a familiar voice (and economy of style), and he both directly and indirectly references *The Loser* throughout.

=

Tudor and Gould both gave up public piano performance in early-to-mid-career around the same time period, the early/mid-1960s. This 'retirement' enabled Gould to pursue his ideals of performance and interpretation in the recording studio, while Tudor did not fully retreat from the concert hall but preoccupied himself with building new instruments and shedding his role of interpreter for that of composer.

Gould was a child prodigy, making his first public performances as a teenager in the mid 1940s. His retirement from the concert hall less than twenty years later allowed him to replace his detested concert hall audience with an idealised, abstract one. Gould perceived the future of music as absolutely dependent upon the progress of recording techniques, of recording as an art form itself with the potential to generate ever more interpretive possibilities and construct performances virtually impossible in a live concert. His investigations resulted in an extremely prolific recorded output.

Tudor had emerged as a virtuoso championing avant-garde music on both sides of the Atlantic in the early 1950s. In the immediate post-war period, the American, German and French avant-garde music worlds were particularly indebted to Tudor, particularly his performances of John Cage's works—many of which were specifically written with him in mind. Tudor became worn out by the constant barrage of young composers expecting him to perform their works. As the drive to perform became increasingly detached from the instrument itself, he too abandoned the classical role of instrumental virtuoso on public view.

Alongside the copious documentation of Gould and Tudor's extremely physical and sensual performance styles, a number of less well-documented rumours recount their supposed impotence, asexuality, and consequent failure in sexual relationships. The bodies of both artists declined very vividly, to a point of flaccidity and fragility which seemed to confirm and complete the escape from their younger virtuoso bodies. Both Gould and Tudor eventually succumbed to strokes, Gould dying from one at the age of 50 in 1982, and Tudor blinded by one before finally passing away at the age of 70 in 1996.

The piano can be variously considered as furniture, totem, trophy, object of devotion and mystical transportation device for elevating and enlightening the listener through the medium of its already-enlightened disciple and channel: the performer. In a (fictional) conceit introduced by Bernhard in *The Loser* and recycled by Gaddis in *Agapē Agape*, Gould *wanted to become the piano*; he didn't want anything to come between him and the music, between him and Bach. For *The Loser*'s other two characters, both close friends of Gould, however, the piano becomes *the enemy*. For them, Gould—and Gould alone— was able to supplicate to the machine and produce his divine music. Again, Tudor's story shadows that of Gould, approximating his role as the idealised performer, interpreter and handmaiden to the work of the contemporary avant-garde. As Tamara Levitz notes, 'Perhaps for this reason, composers always spoke of Tudor as an "instrument" …'[1]

=

> Suicide calculated well in advance, I thought. No spontaneous act of desperation.

So begins the narrator of *The Loser*, referring to the death of Wertheimer, the key 'loser' in the story who explicitly cites Gould's virtuosity—and in particularly his renditions of Bach's *Goldberg Variations*—as the cause of his suicide. This story is related alongside the banal aristocratic upbringing of the narrator, and an essentially fictionalised version of Gould as their fellow student and close friend.

Bernhard's anonymous narrator recounts their schooldays together in the class of Horowitz at the Mozarteum in Salzburg, where he and Wertheimer were the most talented students until they found themselves overshadowed by Gould's genius. They eventually abandon their careers once Glenn destroys their will to become concert virtuosos. Wertheimer goes on to pursue the *human sciences* and eventually isolates himself from the world completely. The narrator himself likewise withdraws from virtuoso performance by giving his Steinway Grand Piano to a music teacher's daughter—not as a selfless act of kindness, but because he knows that she will *destroy the piano with her complete lack of talent!* He then moves to Madrid in order to work on a book provisionally titled 'About Glenn Gould', which never amounts to anything; another failed project. Instead we end up with the story of these three victims of the cruel piano.

> We look at people and we see only cripples, Glenn once said to us, physical or mental and physical, there are no others, I thought. The longer we look at someone the more crippled he appears to us …

Bernhard's characters are also cripples. Wertheimer is the megalomaniacal and depressed control freak who jealously guards and abuses his sister for years until she finally escapes, while the narrator describes his pursuit of a career as a pianist as perversely rooted in his hatred of the family piano's bourgeois symbolism. In a self-conscious *radical act* against his family, the narrator installs a Steinway in the family house, insisting it may only be used for 'artistic purposes' in an attempt to shame the family's existing philistine Ehrbar as mere furniture.

These pathetic characters serve both as personifications of a specific slice of society, and bearers of the vicious weight of Bernhard's renowned vitriol against the broad categories of class, nation-states and the culture industry:

> But Switzerland turns into a deadly prison for all of them, little by little they choke on Switzerland in Switzerland, he could see it, Zizers will kill her, her Swiss husband will kill her, Switzerland will kill her, so he said, I thought.

=

INTERMISSION

I was sat studying some of David Tudor's old papers at one of the tables in the hermetic chamber of the Getty Institute's reading room for archival materials, looking out onto the library stacks. The man across from me was rifling through a box of Fluxus material, and the woman next to me examining some 18th century architectural documents, when I came across these lines at the end of the letter from Cage to Tudor:

> I miss you as much as ever which is a hell of a lot and when I think of music I think of you and vice versa.

I almost burst into tears. It's hard to transmit the emotions felt when facing the remnants of a life spent in so many resonant ways: to further the music of others; to advance the art of instrument construction; to encourage exploration of sound and new technologies …

I sat in the room from morning until closing time copying out pages and pages of Tudor's material—word for word and diagram for diagram. There were piles and piles of notes, some handwritten, others typed, often numerous times, and with constant revisions. The handwritten versions were often on different colours of what was virtually tissue paper, pinks and baby-blues; the typed notes on a rough grade of typing paper; and the musical manuscript paper on Maestro No. 121 14 Plain'.

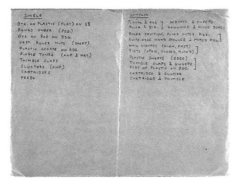

His lists and program notes were also typically copied out numerous times, with a rigorous work ethic evident in the supreme attention to detail and sense of constant tactility. This absolute commitment to the compilation of material made it clear why Tudor was such an ideal instrument for 'indeterminate' composers as Cage, Stockhausen, Cardew, Wolff, and Feldman. The constant revision and reiteration of very slight differences seemed to have been a necessary ritual, through which Tudor achieved the thorough incorporation or embodiment of a piece of music or an intellectual idea.

End of Intermission

=

Glenn Gould's interpretations required a distance from the piano. As he would describe,

> The secret is that you must never move your fingers. If you do so, you will automatically

reflect your most recent tactile configurations that you've been exposed to ... [and later:] I was far from being a slave of the instrument. I tended to learn the score away from the piano. I would learn it completely by memory first ...[2]

Following the withdrawal from public performance, Gould was concerned with the divorce of tactility from the interpretive ideal: how to transport his perfect conception of a piece from his memory to the piano? He practiced less and less in later life, but despite suffering from cramps and other physical conditions which he controlled by various means, it was almost impossible to discern a physical change in his astonishing technical capabilities. His early practice of putting his hands in extremely hot water before playing brought his body into heightened interaction with his mind. He would then typically gesticulate and conduct himself, singing along with his playing, and hovering just inches away from the keyboard, watching his fingers as they seemed to miraculously embody his thinking.

Perhaps the most famous of Gould's rituals, however, was his insistence on bringing his own chair, then taking time to adjust it before sitting down to play. These extra-musical features were criticised and applauded alike, but caused no shortage of fetish appeal for an audience more than willing to buy into the genius myth.

A later, offstage ritual involved trips to several different doctors to receive various medications, each prescribing relief from the side effects of the others' prescriptions. Gould also obsessively notated his eating, sleeping and temperature patterns, as well as his blood pressure and other pathological data. As Bernhard's loser Wertheimer put it, 'Gould *is an art machine*'.

116

In *Agapē Agape* Gaddis's narrator repeatedly returns to the notion of *the detachable self* —a self that can be extrapolated from the body of the narrator in order to observe it. This idea is drawn from Pythagoras's mystical visions, later developed in the esoteric writings of the *Golden Seal*. One of his key ideas is that the self can become memory, and the practice of memory is an act which, once perfected, enables one to *remember the past before existing and the future beyond death*.

As an example of interpretive esotericism, Gould practiced this principle of detachment in his recording, in order to connect two different interpretations of the same piece of music from different days. The one thing they shared was tempo, enabling them to be temporally connected while remaining eternally disjunctive. This mimetic practice allows the meeting of two different points in space and time to co-exist in the fourth dimension in a single moment—then documented 'forever' on an analogue disc, later digitally rendered, re-mastered and so-on.

In Tudor's case, the line between interpreter and composer is a fine one, particularly regarding his performances of Cage 's notoriously indeterminate, graphically-notated scores. Tudor steadfastly refused to concede that he had composed these performances himself, claiming he was simply a faithful—but committed—interpreter:

> I always wanted to be a faithful interpreter and my whole early training was for absolute realization of a score, which is a very complicated proposition. For instance, nowadays, I feel that many people don't read John Cage's score in the sense that they don't realize why the instructions are difficult to understand. Now, when you look at a score that somebody presents to you and you see that you are following the instructions and the way they are laid down, you are the composer's helper. If you have to select a medium for yourself in which to realize those materials, then you have to think about how far you have to go in order to realize it ...[3]

The reproducible performance—of the performer literally *becoming* the piano—had been realised before Gould or Tudor's time in the player piano. The early Welte-Mignon piano, from the beginning of the twentieth century, was able to re-enact the 'recordings' of various virtuoso pianists with incredible accuracy, having patented a recording system which captured the 'touch' and articulation of the pianist to a high degree of sensitivity.

The player piano fused art and industry. Like the virtuoso, it was a self-fulfilling embodiment of the suppression of failure, and the reflexive use of *the instrument itself*—rather than a phonograph, for instance—to reproduce a performance was a major step towards the dislocation of the performer. The 20th century has continually taught us, however, that while technology frequently offers humans prosthetic add-ons, these appendages do not necessarily become replacements.

For Gould, the microphone (another appendage) and other mimetic instruments enabled him to relay his newest and 'freshest' interpretations; for Tudor, amplifiers, tape machines, and homemade electronics allowed composition and interpretation to evolve simultaneously in design and performance. In both cases, this constant reiteration and revision both expressed the implicit concept and embellished the explicit form.

Tudor was interested in developing a system of electronic composition which could ultimately run itself, based on its 'organic' nature. The human element was therefore *pre*-performative, and would otherwise exist only to 'service' the machine, tweaking and coaxing it through the performance. In this sense, the installation and soundcheck were essential aspects of the composition.

Because of his meticulous documentation, Tudor's work can be recreated today. His notes are open and accessible, preoccupied with explaining how the set-ups worked rather than the resulting sound, with the process rather than the (im)material results.[4] In his later years, Tudor's interest in electronic circuitry and instrument construction was paralleled by his love of cooking; the notorious suitcase of cables and gadgets he carted from performance to performance also contained a collection of spices.

Gould's chair and Tudor's suitcase accompanied them to every public appearance. These banal, everyday symbols of work and containment are objects in continual movement. Both carry and substantiate, acting as disembodied, prosthetic parts of the artists' bodies of work.

=

Grieving for the disappearance of failure in the art world, Gaddis concluded with an act of 'failure' itself—the transformation of his life's research into a failed novel—but his ideal of *Agapē* is no less potent for that. As Joseph Tabbi writes:

> *Agapē*—the community of brotherly love celebrated by early Christian writers —has come apart (agape) through mechanization and a technological democracy that reduces art to the level of entertainment, a spectacle for the masses ...

> A capacity for imaginative projection into the life and thought, and language of another person, whether living or dead, through music, literature, the visual arts, a conversation, this is the ethical burden of *agapē* ...

If mass production freed the work of art from its parasitical dependence on the ritual, as Walter Benjamin posited, then what was lost in that deritualisation and yearns to be reclaimed, are storytelling and collective sensory experience. The novels of Bernhard and Gaddis—and the embedded spirits of Gould and Tudor—demonstrate how we might project our imagination and ideas into the lives of others. Their thoughts impregnate our minds with language, images and music. Without them we are doomed to the fate that fusing virtuosity and technology yield, as mourned by Bernhard's loser:

> We aren't people after all, we are art products ...

We are left with the ethical choice that this implies.

CODA

Last year, Sony BMG, recorded a performance of Glenn Gould's 1955 performance of the *Goldberg Variations* in front of a live audience. Yamaha had created a special version of their Diskclavier (a kind of digital player piano) called Zenph™ that could recreate Gould's touch, tempos, dynamics—basically everything except his murmured singing along—and program the entire recording into the piano. The performance took place in the Glenn Gould Studios in Toronto in front of a packed audience. There was a standing ovation for the piano that played 'Glenn'. The re-recording is available for purchase from your favorite record store.

NOTES
1. From the paper 'David Tudor's Corporeal Imagination' presented at the Getty Research Institute Symposium, 'The Art of David Tudor', in 2001.
2. Jonathan Cott, *Conversations with Glenn Gould*, (Chicago: University of Chicago Press, 1984)
3. Quoted from an interview from: Ron Kuivila, 'Open Sources: Words, Circuits and the Notation-Realization Relation in the Music of David Tudor' in *Leonardo Music Journal*, vol. 14, 2004.
4. For example, David Tudor's *Rainforest*. This piece went through multiple versions and is still performed. See John Driscoll and Matt Rogalsky, 'David Tudor's Rainforest: An Evolving Exploration of Resonance' in *Leonardo Music Journal*, vol. 14, 2004.

REFERENCES
—Bernhard, Thomas, *The Loser* (New York: Knopf, 1991), translated by Jack Dawson. Originally published as *Der Untergeher* (1983)
—Gaddis, William, *Agapē Agape* (New York: Viking Press, 2002)

as in VOYAGES: Parnet announces this title by saying that it's the demonstration of a concept as a paradox because Deleuze invented the concept, nomadism, but he hates traveling. Deleuze says he doesn't like the conditions of travel for a poor intellectual. It means going to conferences, at the other end of the world, and talking-before and a talking-after with people who greet you quite kindly, and a talking-after with people who listened to you quite politely, talk talk talk, Deleuze says. So, for him, an intellectual's travel is the opposite of traveling. Go to the ends of the earth to talk, that is, to do something one can do at home, and to see people and talking before, talking after, this is a monstrous voyage.

THE FREEDOM OF NEGATIVE EXPRESSION

by
Chris Evans

Viewing Draft

TITLE SEQUENCE:
FADE IN

          ARTIST 1
    is a nihilist

FADE OUT
FADE IN

          ARTIST 2
    is a former member of the
    British Constructivists

FADE OUT
FADE IN

    Together they are making
    THE FREEDOM OF NEGATIVE EXPRESSION

FADE OUT

EXT. AN EXIT TO THE BARBICAN, LONDON
Grey evening light.

THE NIHILIST, a well-heeled man in his early 30s, is leaving
the Barbican from one of the exits. He puts on headphones,
places a hand in his jacket pocket and switches on his mp3
player. We hear music that could be considered as being
'nihilist'. Our POV is from behind THE NIHILIST as the camera
follows his route back to his apartment, through dilapidated
housing estates and eventually to a gated apartment block. The
music on THE NIHILIST'S headphones provides the soundtrack to
the journey. THE NIHILIST takes the lift to his apartment.

INT. BOURGEOIS BOHEMIAN INTERIOR

The lift doors open directly to THE NIHILIST's apartment. We
see an expansive living area with two partially open doors: one
leading to a kitchen, the other to the artist's studio. THE
NIHILIST walks to a table where a phone is ringing. We don't
hear the phone, we are still hearing the music on his headphones. The music continues as he starts talking on the phone.
THE NIHILIST reaches into his pocket and switches off his mp3
player, there's a moment of interference on the phoneline and
we come into the conversation halfway through.

As THE NIHTLIST talks he picks up and plays with various
objects in the apartment. Our POV is moving, following him
around the apartment. CUs on his face, eyes, phone etc. and on
symbolic objects in the apartment which should be intercut
whenever THE BRITISH CONSTRUCTIVIST is speaking. Throughout the
film, until the closing dialogue, THE NIHILIST appears restless
and distracted.
                    THE NIHILIST
(holding an empty wineglass up to the light, or some other
transparent object)
                        But then how would you explain the prismatic
                        play of opacity and translucency in your
                        early work, particularly the work you were
                        making in the mid 60s?

Throughout the reply, THE NIHILIST walks around the apartment,

listening, holding the glass. The camera pans, revealing that
the opening shot was seen in a mirror hanging on one wall.

THE BRITISH CONSTRUCTIVIST
(we hear her voice on the phone)

> I always say I believe in transparency. Not
> reflection. Reflection is random, it mirrors
> whatever's happening in the room. And yet it
> is a double fraud in that it simultaneously
> suggests the illusion of depth. Transparency
> is the sincere attempt at depth, as opposed
> to staged depth, it's an attempt to see
> through the surface into the sub-mediatic
> sphere. To put it this way is to understand
> how this imperfect allegory of the conspira-
> cy, or the world system itself, offers the
> best representational potential. Established,
> official narratives have never been much good
> at conveying the collective, well... except
> in the explosive drama of war and revolution.
> And yet, unfortunately, the cognitive poten-
> tial of real transparency must be for the
> most part an unconscious one, for it is only
> at that deeper level of our fantasy that we
> think about the social system in any realis-
> tic way, and sense those realities that are
> too horrific to behold otherwise.

THE NIHILIST
(puts down the glass. looks in mirror as he speaks to his own
reflection. This is the first time that we see him head-on)

> Yes, and, through our collaboration, I am
> sure that we can sense this horrific reality,
> describe it, give it form... Give it form
> that is the perfect inverse of the pointless
> affirmation of reflection. I agree with
> Borges — that mirrors and copulation are
> obscene, because they increase the number of
> men. I have myself made certain forays into
> the art of the 'vanitas', the reflected
> image, the painted skull, the imaginary mean-

> ingfulness of death, if only to exorcise its hold over me. The mirror's illusion of depth is of no use to us, because it is already filled with an image of the world.

THE NIHILIST turns, looks around the room, at the TV etc. Cut in with intense CU of the things he is looking at, TV, furniture, objets d'art etc.

THE NIHILIST

(continuing from previous dialogue)

> Your idea of transparency allows us to escape from that, allows us to see through the disguise of reality, the theatre of media events, the fiction of history that blocks our vision. Perhaps the surface of the world system is in fact a window onto the emptiness that lies behind it, an emptiness that can only acquire real meaning in the context of the unending, blind conspiracy that ceaselessly attempts to block it out behind the walls of a hall of mirrors.

While THE NIHILIST is still listening on the telephone, he looks out of the window. Cut to view from window - faked if necessary

THE BRITISH CONSTRUCTIVIST

> But that is unfashionable as a theory, very unfashionable as a thought even. To indulge in any cognitive function of the conspiratorial plot you must be able to flicker in and out, like a pathetic old broken down TV. This is why I've preferred to use glass of varying degrees of translucency. To underline this surreptitious attempt at depth. Some curators, some critics, some dealers, some historians think they can be so bloody transparent just by being so bloody coquettish and selfcritical. Can an exhibition really be critical of the art that's in it?

THE NIHILIST turns away from window, sits down on a piece of modernist furniture.

                    THE NIHILIST
(talking almost to his feet but gesturing expansively)
                         I have come to see the public exhibition as
                         an endpoint, like the event horizon of a
                         black hole, the moment at which any hope for
                         transcendence, all the grand ambitions that
                         artists have for their work, are sacrificed
                         on the altar of reality — forced into being
                         and so, at the same moment, destroyed.
                         Destroyed by the reality of their public
                         existence, of their capitulation to the mean-
                         ingless regime of culture that limits and
                         contains them. But sure, you can persuade
                         your audience that you are giving them some-
                         thing of value. These art lovers have already
                         left part of their reason behind, and any
                         vaudeville hypnotist could finish the job.
                         Their culture restricts them so completely
                         that they will see what they came to see —
                         an empty affirmation of their own taste and
                         privilege.

THE NIHILIST stands up, struck by an idea.

                    THE NIHILIST
(continuing from previous dialogue)
                         But this is something that we can use. Take
                         their bourgeois tastes, with all of their
                         meaninglessness, and sell those back to them
                         at a hundred times the price. Our taste — I
                         mean their taste — in furniture, in fashion,
                         in the colours of their cars, the way they
                         smile. The way that they are happy to look
                         into the mirror of themselves — to enjoy the
                         concrete manifestation of the means of pro-
                         duction that allows them to exist and at the
                         same time limits what they can be — and call
                         that culture.

As THE BRITISH CONTRUCTIVIST replies, THE NIHILIST walks into
his studio (the camera doesn't follow him - our POV is
restricted to seeing his profile through the partially opened
door). CU of THE NIHILIST's face as he looks at his artwork in
progress, he has a dead-pan expression. He then leaves his studio, with the door still ajar, goes into the kitchen and opens
a bottle of wine, still listening on the phone.

> THE BRITISH CONSTRUCTIVIST
> Yes, we can see there are limits here, and
> this access to the mechanisms that affirm the
> bourgeoisie's existing image of themselves is
> always a class issue as well. Not only in
> terms of access to education. But also in
> terms of a creative class bred and raised by
> people who can only allow for a tightly cir-
> cumscribed economy of mix'n'rule. Of course,
> the artworld is particularly interesting for
> minorities and all the other downtrodden
> since it offers not only apparently, seeming-
> ly, ostensibly uncodified rules of entry, but
> also the transitional possibilities of menial
> jobs within its very core. Assistantships,
> technical responsibilities, etc. In other
> words, you're browbeaten and used more easi-
> ly, and even peabrains such as Brian
> O'Doherty could come up with slogans like
> "art is the opiate of the upper middle class-
> es". And artists are such typical examples of
> the tension and pretension of the rising mid-
> dle classes themselves. Which doesn't keep
> them from policing all sorts of boundaries
> within their own little playpens.

Whilst THE BRITISH CONSTRUCTIVIST is speaking, THE NIHILIST
comes out of the kitchen holding the opened bottle of wine.
He puts the wine down on a small coffee table and, with his
free hand, turns off the lights, listens in the dark for a
few seconds (black screen). He turns the lights back on then
absent-mindedly turns them off and on again.

                    THE BRITISH CONSTRUCTIVIST
(continuing previous dialogue)
                         Did you ever notice the self-congratulating
                         way political artists who belong to the elite
                         arena of the transnational art world react in
                         front of hardcore political activists — those
                         who wear ugly Oxfam pants and first degree
                         unironic Che Guevara T-Shirts? Have you ever
                         watched?

THE NIHILIST sits down again, pouring himself a glass of wine.

                         THE NIHILIST
                         I must confess that I have never had this
                         experience at first hand, but I suspect it is
                         similar to the way that some of my Swiss
                         friends graciously forgive the teenage snow-
                         boarders for sneaking on to the piste without
                         paying, because it gives them a feeling of
                         superiority and a little extra cultural
                         cachet at the same time.

THE NIHILIST raises his glass.

                         THE NIHILIST
(continuing from previous dialogue)
                         They can enjoy playing the bohemian, because
                         they know that their bourgeois citadel is not
                         under any real threat.

The phone connection breaks while THE NIHILIST is talking.

                         THE NIHILIST
(continuing from previous dialogue)
                              Hello?
                              Hello?

THE NIHILIST re-dials and, without commenting on being cut off
THE BRITISH CONSTRUCTIVIST immediately starts speaking. THE
NIHILIST is sipping wine and nodding.

THE BRITISH CONSTRUCTIVIST
The real boundaries, the real conflicts of
interest, used to be more transparent. 19th
century art bohemia really was explicitly and
officially weak, in terms of class background
and cultural capital. This spawned an adver-
sity to the salons, and any type of subsidised art — even if this subsidised art was
rabidly anti-bourgeois. And so today of
course the loss of the bourgeois hold over
museums is an opportunity. But for whom? How
can we discern who is gaining from all this?

Pause while THE NIHILIST swallows wine and thinks. he stands up
again and begins to walk around, glass in hand]

THE NIHILIST
And how can we turn this unknown possibility
into a real opportunity? If these possibilities exist, perhaps we can use them to demonstrate the futile nature of this process of
reconfiguration. Yes, I'm sure that we can
work this concept into our proposal. But how
do we discern the best way to proceed? Who
should I call?

THE NIHILIST looks for and finds a notebook and a pen during
this, and begins to make notes.

THE BRITISH CONSTRUCTIVIST
Any science of cultural production implies
the study of the field with respect to powerful decision makers — official and unofficial
— and the development of this position over
time. And also a study of the internal structure of the field, of the competitions for
legitimacy between various positions, official and unofficial. And above all, of the
genesis of the habitus of the holders of
these various positions as well.

                    THE NIHILIST
          Sorry, I missed that.

                    THE BRITISH CONSTRUCTIVIST
          There's a big and desperate need for both
          microinstitutional studies of subject forma-
          tion, as well as macrostructural studies of
          exploitation, along with genealogical studies
          to see shifts in time. That is the only way
          we can see through the servile virtuosity
          that has come over us. That has beset us.
          At least we used to be able to see the
          rules, and thus at rare moments the struc-
          tures behind these rules, but today we do not
          even see the rules, only the individuals who
          represent them, the curators, directors, col-
          lectors, sponsors, editors, and the dance of
          servile virtuosity begins.

THE NIHILIST, excited, closes the notebook

                    THE NIHILIST
          Yes — and this is our subject, of course.
          Those servile virtuosos who believed that
          they were doing something. With their empty
          forms and their radical words, always affirm-
          ing, always believing that they were moving
          forward, while all the time they are just
          being whirled around in this endless dance
          that ceaselessly returns to its starting
          point. Courbet and Manet. Malevich and
          Picasso. Pollock and Newman. Perhaps, despite
          themselves, they have already achieved the
          freedom of negative expression, perhaps they
          have already unknowingly done what we are
          trying to do?

                    THE BRITISH CONSTRUCTIVIST
          Who knows Barnett Newman anymore, who knows
          Monica Ross? And John Ahearn must lose. He is
          doomed to lose. I think it was he who said:

"One should have no illusions. Until capitalism and imperialism are brought down, cultural institutions will go on being, in their
primary role, lapdogs of a system that
spreads misery and death to people everywhere
on the planet." And turning to the UK in
particular, how come we have these didactic,
compensatory approaches in art in this country? Is that a mere coincidence?

THE NIHILIST puts down the phone, we continue to hear THE
BRITISH CONSTRUCTIVIST's voice. THE NIHILIST starts constructing experimental maquettes out of household objects. Our POV is
with the partially open door to the studio in the background.
We can see evidence of fabrication: a maquette, plaster, brass
rods etc.

                    THE BRITISH CONSTRUCTIVIST
(continuing from previous dialogue)
                         Who still remembers the Athenaeum movements
                         in Liverpool and elsewhere? Art as a means to
                         resolve social differences by fostering the
                         common pursuit of profit, rational amusement
                         and mental improvement. This was distinctive-
                         ly English as an approach. And I'm not saying
                         the Russians did it better, or had it better,
                         or that Malevich or the constructivists were
                         innocent. There were various collusions, var-
                         ious complicities between the Russian avant-
                         garde and the politburo. The shared effort to
                         breed a New Man, that secular eschatology
                         that was to buttress "Stalinism" one day.
                         Stalinism which was nothing other than a
                         faithful realization of militant avant-garde
                         hubris. Stalinist constructivism triumphed in
                         some places, CIA-funded abstract expression-
                         ism in others.

THE NIHILIST walks over to his expensive hi-fi system and
presses play. We hear the first bars of the same 'nihilist'
music that we heard in the opening scene. We also hear THE

BRITISH CONSTRUCTIVIST continuing to speak.

> THE BRITISH CONSTRUCTIVIST
(continuing from previous dialogue)
>> It will take a long time before we can decide on the enduring outcome of the ideological struggles between socialism and capitalism that took place over the 20th century. The reason for this is that the influence of intellectuals and the bourgeoisie stemming from the preceding struggles and societies, along with their social ideologies, will exist for a long time yet. If we don't grasp this fully, or worse, if we do not grasp it at all, one runs the risk of misconceiving the importance of struggle on an ideological level.

> THE NIHILIST
(looking down, until now he has appeared restless and distracted – but now he appears resolute and decisive)
>> Yes, exactly.

Short pause. THE NIHILIST looks up directly at the camera.

> THE NIHILIST
>> And it is the image of this unknown future, this void into which our efforts in the present will undoubtedly fall, that we must describe in order to realise The Freedom of Negative Expression as an image of both the constant, unwinnable struggle against the unfolding of future events, and of the false consciousness of our own time.

FADE OUT

FADE IN
> THE END

FADE OUT

NOT AN 'SS'

by Louis Lüthi

Really, now! If even the exceptions weren't
true, what *could* you trust?
(Gustave Flaubert, *Bouvard and Pécuchet*)

The origin and uses of the 'ß' or 'sharp s' seem
to be as surprisingly equivocal as the paths
used by type designers to outline the ligature
are diverse. In German its numerous epithets,
varying from region and age of speaker, include:
*Eszett, scharfes S, Ringel-S, Dreierles-S, Doppel-S,
Buckel-S, Straßen-S* and *Rucksack-S*. Outside of
German-speaking countries it is often mistaken
for an uppercase 'B', lowercase beta ('β') or even
a cursive Cyrillic Ve ('в'); a quick internet search
reveals it to be alternately referred to as 'that
funny looking B','a version of the greek character
beta' and 'one cool little squiggle'.

The Brockhaus dictionary definition of the
Eszett dates the 'ß' from the 14th century ligature
of blackletter 'long s' ('ſ') and 'tailed z' ('ȝ').
The renowned German typographer Jan
Tschichold, on the other hand, confidently
demonstrated it to be a combination of 'long s'
and 'short s' ('s') by illustrating the fusion of the
two letters into the one glyph we know today.[1]
Yet neither explanation is entirely satisfactory.
Tschichold's argument was based purely on
typographic reasoning and has, it seems, no
linguistic validation and it is difficult to visually
correspond the Brockhaus definition to its purely
typographic terms. In all likelihood a combination
of unclear factors including the possible
blackletter use of 'tailed z' instead of 'long s' in
the terminal position of words or morphemes,
coupled with its subsequent adjustment for roman
typefaces, resulted in the contemporary shape
and use of the 'ß'.[2]

Therefore the *Eszett* is, misleadingly, not
simply a combination of *Es* ('s') and *Zett* ('z')
and it has nothing at all to do with the number
'3'—other than a passing visual resemblance
—as insinuated by the primarily Swabian dialect
Dreierles-S. The description *scharfes S* ('sharp
s') is in this sense more accurate, as it at least
phonetically approximates the symbol, while the
Swiss plain *Doppel-S* ('double s') is technically
correct, but not all the time nor everywhere:

although the 'ß' is obsolete in Switzerland as
well as Liechtenstein and also regarded as an 'ss'
in collation, the latest German Spelling Reform
initiated in 1996 clearly states that in Germany
and Austria 'ss' should be used after a short vowel
and 'ß' following a long vowel or dipthong.[3]

Moreover, because the *Eszett* is solely
—perhaps uniquely so?—a lowercase character,
these (partial) misnomers have affected the
setting of words in all capitals. Usually 'ß'
is rendered capital 'SS' as it should be, but
sometimes one sees 'SZ' mistakenly used instead.
Several type designers over the years have
attempted to introduce a majuscule *Eszett* to avoid
this discrepancy, with the latest unsuccessful
proposal dating from 2004.[4] As a result one does
occasionally see a customized majuscule 'ß' used
or a miniscule 'ß' stubbornly squeezed between
broader capital letters. Only rarely does one
comes across a capital 'B' used in place of either
(perhaps the plastic letter set or sticker sheet
didn't include enough characters, or the text
conversion malfunctioned, or someone unfamiliar
with German misread/typed it, etc.).

The design of the ligature itself is even often
noticeably unwieldy for type designers. The
illustration on the overleaf shows a composite
'ß' made up of Mac OS 9 standard system
typefaces. In it can be seen a wealth of variations
in proportion and detail: some tend towards
a rounded, barely incomplete 'B' while others
closely approach the contours of a 'β'. The
inclusion of a short horizontal stroke at the x-
height of the left ascender—a remnant of the
'long s'—is a final inconsistency, a detail left to
the discretion of type designers.

Words, it is generally accepted, can be open
to interpretation, but letters are more or less
taken to be fixed entities, akin to indestructible
little atoms. A same letter can of course
represent different sounds, or remain legible
in various forms, but the idea of a letter being
even slightly equivocal—in origin, name and
use—is somehow more striking than the idea of
a word being so. The *Eszett* is remarkable in this
aspect and it emphasizes that misunderstandings
and ambiguities of signs form as much a
part of language and communication as the
straightforward and indisputable.

There are several letters, ligatures or combinations of letters and diacritics in the Latin
alphabet that have become synonymous with
an entire language; the Dutch *lange ij* ('ij') and
the Spanish *eñe* ('ñ') are two examples. Such

132

alphabetical variations form a sort of shorthand, clichéd yet nonetheless effective, to relate to a language and/or culture: an entirely white frame in an *Astérix* comic book containing only an onomatopoeic 'Wøøf!' in a speech bubble is sufficient to place the setting in wintry Scandinavia, for example. In a similar way, the ligature 'ß' has come, to a certain extent, to represent the identity of the German language and any attempt to diminish or abolish its use is met with some opposition in Germany and Austria. This was evident after the introduction of the German Spelling Reform in 1996, which dealt with, among larger reforms pertaining to syllabification and punctuation, clarifying and limiting the use of the *Eszett*. Such was the hostile reception to the overall proposed changes that an amended version of the Reform only finally came into effect in 2006.[5]

As the 'ß' is a unique, traditional feature of the German language (that is, when it is recognized as such abroad), so too it may conversely seem an anachronistic element in international forums such as the internet. Although the predominant use of the Unicode character encoding scheme by computers theoretically enables it to be consistently written and read with most software, it is not always taken into account. For instance, it is not yet possible to register domain names including 'ß' (or any accents or ligatures for that matter) and an internet search of 'ß' results in many 'SS' links, somewhat unfortunately. The early IBM DOS code page even conflated the *Eszett* and the beta as one hybrid character[6] —a seemingly innocent error, like assuming an 'ß' is simply an 'ss'.

This piece first appeared under the title 'Not a B', in a special issue of *02* magazine, summer 2007, pp. 50–53. With thanks to Anthony Huberman.

NOTES
1. Jan Tschichold, *Meisterbuch der Schrift*, 2nd edn. (Ravensburg: Maier, 1965)
2. For a detailed account of this hypotheses in all its linguistic and phonetic subtleties, see: Prof. Dr Herbert E. Brekle, 'Zur handschriftlichen und typographischen Geschichte der Buchstabenligatur ß aus gotisch-deutschen und humanistisch-italienischen Kontexten', in *Gutenberg Jahrbuch 2001*. Mainz: 2001, pp. 67–76.
3. Dagmar Giersberg, *The End of the Debate*. See: http://www.goethe.de/kue/lit/dos/dds/en630493.htm
4. See: *SIGNA, Beitrage zur Signographie*, nr. 9, 'Das große Eszett', in *Pegau*, March 2006.
5. See note 3.
6. See: http://en.wikipedia.org/wiki/ß

W

as in WITTGENSTEIN: Parnet says she knows he's nothing for Deleuze, but it's only a word. Deleuze says, he doesn't like to talk about that, it's a philosophical catastrophe. It's the very type of a 'school', a regression of all philosophy, a massive regression. Deleuze considers the Wittgenstein matter to be quite sad. They imposed [ils ont foutu] a system of terror in which, under the pretext of doing something new, it's poverty introduced as grandeur.

X Y

Parnet says that X is unknown and Y is unspeakable [indicible] [Deleuze is laughing], so they move on directly to the final letter of the alphabet …

Z

as in ZIGAZAG: Parnet says they are at the final letter, Zed, and Deleuze says, 'Just in time!' Parnet says that it's not the Zed of Zorro the Lawman [le Justicier], since Deleuze has expressed throughout the alphabet how much he doesn't like judgment. It's the Zed of bifurcation, of lightning, it's the letter that one finds in the names of great philosophers: Zen, Zarathoustra, Leibniz, Nietzsche, Spinoza, BergZon [Deleuze laughs], and of course, Deleuze. Deleuze laughs, saying she has been very witty with BergZon and very kind toward Deleuze himself. He considers Zed to be a great letter that establishes a return to A, the fly, the zigging movement of the fly, the Zed, the final word, no word after zigzag. Deleuze thinks it's good to end on this word.

DOT DOT DOT 14
Summer 2007
ISBN-13: 978-90-77620-08-3

© 2007 Dexter Sinister.
All rights reserved.
All material is compiled
from sources believed to
be reliable, but published
without responsibility
for errors or omissions.

Published twice a year
by Dexter Sinister
38 Ludlow Street (Basement)
New York, NY 10002
U.S.A.
www.dextersinister.org
info@dextersinister.org

<editor@dot-dot-dot.nl>
www.dot-dot-dot.nl

EDITOR
Stuart Bailey
<sinister@o-r-g.com>
New York

This issue co-edited with
David Reinfurt
<reinfurt@o-r-g.com>
New York

Production/Coordination:
Sarah Crowner
<sarah@dextersinister.org>

THANKS
Mai Abu ElDahab
Peter Bilak
Jason Fulford
Anthony Huberman
Virginija Januskeviciute
Tony Law
Petra Cerne Oven
Joke Robard
Frances Stark
Thea Westreich/T.W.A.A.S.
Felix Weigand
Werkplaats Typografie
Luke Wood

PRINTING
Logotipas, Vilnius, Lithuania

DDD has attempted to
contact all copyright holders,
but this has not been possible
in all instances. We apologise
for any omissions and,
if noted, will amend in any
future editions.

Shadow cover based on an
unused *Cabinet* magazine
proposal; reproduced with
due respect and thanks in
advance retrospect.

CONTRIBUTORS

Justin Beal
Los Angeles

Chris Evans
Berlin

Ryan Gander
London

Rob Giampietro
New York

Melissa Gronlund
London

Will Holder
London

Christoph Keller
Eigeltingen-Münchof

Robin Kinross
London

Louis Lüthi
Amsterdam

Graham Meyer
Philadelphia

John Morgan
London

Emily Pethick
Utrecht

Radim Peško
Amsterdam

Steve Rushton
Rotterdam

Dmitri Siegel
Philadelphia

Howard Singerman
Charlottesville

Alex Waterman
New York

Mark Wigley
New York

Stephen Willats
London

All pieces designed by
editors/authors except
'The Middle of Nowhere' and
'The Freedom of Negative
Expression' by Will Holder;
and 'I.U.(3)' by John Morgan.

'A Rear Guard' was originally
written for *ŠMC/CAC Interviu*,
no. 7–8, summer 2008.
Reproduced with thanks.

DISPERSION

DDD is available
foremost from our own
point of distribution:
Dexter Sinister
Just-In-Time Workshop
& Occasional Bookstore
38 Ludlow Street (Basement)
New York, NY 10002
U.S.A.
*Open Saturdays from
12 to 6 pm*
www.dextersinister.org
info@dextersinister.org

SUBSCRIPTIONS
1 year (2 issues):
€29 in Europe
€44 everywhere else
(worldwide exchange rates
subject to change) from:
Bruil & Van de Staaij
Postbus 75,
7940 AB Meppel
The Netherlands
T: +31 522 261 303
F: +31 522 257 827
info@bruil.info
www.bruil.info

DISTRIBUTION EUROPE
Coen Sligting Bookimport
Van Oldenbarneveldtstraat 77
1052 JW Amsterdam
The Netherlands
T: +31 20 673 2280
F: +31 20 664 0047
sligting@xs4all.nl

DISTRIBUTION UK
Central Books
115 Wallis Road
London E9 5LN
UK
T: +44 (0)845 458 9911
F: +44 (0)845 458 9912
orders@centralbooks.com
www.centralbooks.com

DISTRIBUTION AMERICAS,
ASIA, AFRICA, AUSTRALIA
Princeton Architectural Press
37 E 7th Street
New York, NY 10003
USA
T: +1 212 995 9620
F: +1 212 995 9454
sales@papress.com
www.papress.com

ADVERTISING
DDD adverts are paid
according to the background
greyscale percentage;
contact <crowner@o-r-g.com>
for rates or reservations

CREDITS

Stephen Willats images:

p. 94: *Homeostatic Drawing
No. 1*, 1968, 60 × 71 cm,
pencil on paper; *Organic
Exercise No. 1*, Series 1,
1962, 61 × 76 cm, pencil
on paper

p. 95: *Five Acts of Transformation*, 1998, 53.5 × 82 cm,
ink, pencil, Letraset on
paper

p. 96: *Complex World*, 1999,
59.5 × 84 cm, ink, Letraset
on paper

p. 98: *A Model of Perceptual
Transformation*, 1978,
64 × 90 cm, watercolour, ink,
gouache, Letraset on paper

p. 99: *Multiple Clothing,
Creative Noise*, October
1997, 42.5 × 64 cm, poster
paint, ink, Letraset on paper
(courtesy the artist)

p. 101: *Encounter In
The Corridor*, February
1991, 84 × 59 cm wide.
Photographic prints, acrylic
paint, ink, Letraset on
card (courtesy the artist
and Galerie Lumen Travo,
Amsterdam)

p. 102: *Moving Between
The Past Present And Future*,
July–January 1996, 3
panels, each panel 81.5 ×
112 cm, photographic prints,
photographic dye, acrylic
paint, ink, Letraset on card
(courtesy the artist and
the Victoria Miro Gallery,
London)

p. 103: *Street Talk,
Amsterdam*, September–
December 2004, 2 panel
work, each panel 70 × 155
cm, photographic prints,
photographic dye, acrylic
paint, ink, Letraset on
card (courtesy the artist
and Galerie Lumen Travo,
London)

p. 104: *The World As It Is
And The World As It Could
Be* (2006), 125 × 82 cm, ink,
pencil, Letraset on paper
(courtesy the artist and
the Victoria Miro Gallery
London)

YALE UNIVERSITY SCHOOL OF ART

ASSISTANT PROFESSOR OF GRAPHIC DESIGN
Salary approximately $65,000. To begin
July 1, 2008. 3 year full time ladder appointment.
Primary responsibilities include teaching,
committee work within the School of Art and
participation in the continuing development
of undergraduate and graduate classes in the
graphic design study area. Participation is
required in a variety of aspects in the life of the
School including individual and group critiques
within the area as well as interdisciplinary
critiques. We require an MFA with experience
teaching beyond the TA level and an equivalent
level of professional work. Include a letter of
application and a current resume, 20 images on
CD or DVD, and a description of the ideas that
inform your own work. Provide us with the
names of three persons from whom letters of
reference may be obtained and a self addressed,
stamped envelope for return of materials.
A/D October 12, 2007.

Sheila Levrant de Bretteville,
Director, Graphic Design Search,
Yale University School of Art, PO Box 208339,
New Haven, CT 06520-8339.

Yale values diversity in its faculty and students
and especially encourages applications from
women and underrepresented minorities.
Yale University is an affirmative action/equal
opportunities employer.

CALARTS

WWW. COIFFEURNYC. COM

Le coiffeur des artistes

TINKER TAILOR
SOLDIER SAILOR
RICH MAN POOR MAN
BEGGAR MAN THIEF

Werkplaats Typografie
Agnietenplaats 2
6822 JD Arnhem
tel: +31 (0)26 3535774
www.werkplaatstypografie.org
mail@werkplaatstypografie.org

LINETO.COM

ABCDEFGHIJKLMNOPQRSTUVWXYZ
abcdefghijklmnopqrstuvwxyz
ÄÁÀÂÇÆÆËÉÊÏÍÎÔÓÒÕØŒÑÜÚÙÛŸ
äáàâãçæëéèêïíîöóòôõøœñüúùûÿ
1234567890()[]{}<>≤≥
"" ' ` ‚ „"‚'«»‹›^ˆˇ ~
¿¡?:„· ...*/|\±+–——_ ≈≠÷ ♀
$¢£¥#@%‰&Ə®©TMao ßðſ fifl°° ¶†‡